The Careers Adviser's Guide

The Careers Adviser's Guide

How to Give Practical Job Search Advice to Clients

Rebecca Corfield

First published in 1995

Kogan Page Limited
120 Pentonville Road
London N1 9JN

British Library Cataloguing in Publication Data

A CIP record for this book is available from the British Library.

ISBN 0–7494 –1222–4

Typeset by Saxon Graphics Ltd, Derby
Printed and bound in Great Britain by Clays Ltd, St Ives plc

To Matt

Acknowledgements

Many people have helped me to put this book together but special thanks go to Lesley Anderson, Barbara Bishop, Robin Charnley, Brendan Tarring and Pat White for the insights they shared with me.

Contents

'Careers advisers help to draw the map but the client chooses the destination and the route' Freelance careers consultant

Introduction

'The right role for an adviser is to facilitate and empower, not to solve. That is the client's responsibility.' **Careers guidance trainer**

I have been advising individuals and groups about the direction that their careers should take for the last ten years. Initially I worked as a careers officer with a local education authority and advised young people in schools and colleges. Then I moved to work with adult clients, particularly those looking for work after a period of unemployment. I saw that the problems facing people in their career choice are mostly the same whatever their age. They need information and help to weigh up the options available and then encouragement and advice to follow their chosen path, or to amend it as necessary.

Today, the world of careers advice is opening up. It is now no longer a dimly remembered, hidden and slightly mysterious activity which takes place in a remote and normally unused interview room down a dark corridor at school. In the past, the only people who dispensed careers advice were those who had completed a two-year training complete with intensive monitoring and feedback on their performance. Nowadays, more and more people are finding that they need to know about career development and it is becoming a more regular and accessible feature of modern life.

Television programmes, careers items in glossy magazines, information freely available from different employers and a host of companies and institutions offering help with career planning, mean that careers guidance is finally coming of age. It is no longer just the realm of the careers officer working with school-age young people, but represents an increasing concern to many different organisations and individuals. With the current high rates of unemployment there are many people who want to be able to give advice about the best way to find work, and are keen to be able to help others with their future plans.

Even with the increased interest in career development and the plethora of organisations and individuals now involved in its promulgation, it is still a slightly secret activity, normally carried out in private or in small groups, and with the information and advice kept private. This makes it quite difficult for those who have not received advice to imagine exactly what goes on. I am often asked how to train staff in the rudiments of careers advice. Although there is no substitute for a thorough training course, not everyone needs to be an expert in the subject. Some people work on the fringes of giving advice, perhaps alongside professional advisers, or are only asked about vocational subjects as a small part of their job, and would like more of an insight into what the work involves.

The Careers Adviser's Guide sums up the advice I would give to those who have an interest in careers guidance and want to know what the major issues are. It will provide you with a quick and handy introduction to the basics of the work with a clear plan to follow for giving good guidance, whatever the circumstances in which it is needed.

This book is aimed at anybody who is concerned with the career choices of young people and adults. It will help you if you are a careers officer, adviser, school teacher or concerned parent, if you work alongside careers advisers or write on careers subjects and want to know more about the work. Perhaps you are considering undergoing a professional training course and want to understand what the job and the training involves. College counsellors, trainers, tutors and subject teachers will all gain an insight into the complex world of careers guidance. You may work for a Training and

Enterprise Council or Local Enterprise Company, in a Jobcentre, or run a Jobclub, you may be a youth worker or social worker, personnel officer or business adviser. If your life or work ever involves questions about career development, you may find ideas to help you in this book.

The clients with whom you are concerned may include school pupils, family members, young people at youth clubs, college students, school and college leavers, people on training schemes, those who are unemployed, women returners, job changers, those trying to develop their career, redundant employees and those seeking self-employment, part-time work or voluntary work. You may give advice to others in a social setting, may charge a fee for your service or may be funded to provide guidance to those without the resources to pay. Careers guidance takes place in all these guises and situations and many more besides.

You can see from the above list of possible readers that there is now a huge number of people who are expected to be knowledgeable about careers and are also supposed to be able to communicate their ideas to other people. While there is a lot of information on different career choices provided by careers publishers and different industries, there is a great lack of information for those people who advise on careers. Because of my previous books, '*Preparing Your Own CV*', '*Successful Interview Skills*' and '*How You Can Get That Job!*', I am often asked how advisers can use the systems I describe with their clients. The world of work now offers increasingly complex choices for clients and their helpers. I wanted to help the new or uncertain advisers to find the answers to their questions and check out their approach to the job.

This book aims to be a tool which you can use to help you carry out your work better, whether you need it in a formal setting or just as a guide for more informal careers advice. If you are a beginner in the field of advising others, and have recently acquired this responsibility, you will find down-to-earth practical tips to increase your confidence and enable you to work effectively.

How to get the most out of this book

We have established that for some reason you have an interest in careers guidance. Perhaps you need to be able to start advising people as part of your working life, or perhaps you are just keen to know more about how career decisions are made and the best way to aid that process. This book is written to guide you in the first steps towards giving good careers guidance as well as acting as a refresher to those with prior knowledge. It may be that since your training in vocational guidance you have become stuck in a rut and want to use this book to remind you of the basic principles and inspire you with the bigger picture of what guidance is all about.

The first chapter of this book explains the different styles of interviewing that are possible. Advisers are not machines which always perform in the same manner; their roles can change either according to the situation in which they find themselves, the clients with whom they are dealing or their own personality. Some styles are more appropriate for certain circumstances and we shall explore the effect of these different styles both on the client and on the guidance process. You can identify your own preferred style. As an adviser you have certain responsibilities to your clients but you can also expect standards of behaviour back in return and this chapter outlines such interrelationships.

The different problems and attitudes presented by the client are the subject of Chapter 2. Understanding how the client is feeling and what he or she is thinking is the secret of being a useful adviser. We shall look behind the issues that the client presents and explore some of the deeper worries which afflict people about their career options. Clients have rights in a professional relationship but they also have some responsibilities to their adviser. We look at both in this chapter.

Chapter 3, on career choice, will examine the different modern theories about career development. What do the experts think about how we decide on our career choice? Can their ideas help us as advisers? How should we perform our role as advisers once we know about these different ideas around career development? Chapter 4 examines some of the ways that careers advisers have developed in order to best facilitate clients' understanding of themselves. Types of tests are covered as well as some helpful exercises to try with clients.

Apart from giving careers information and helping clients to understand the options open to them, one of the most useful types of assistance that can be given concerns job applications. Often we need to be confident about advising people how to present themselves on paper using CVs and covering letters. There is a CV questionnaire in Chapter 5 with which you can test your own understanding of the issues. Application forms can be difficult enough for us to complete, never mind advise other people about. This chapter gives you a complete understanding of what will impress employers and help you to assist your clients effectively.

Clients also often need to know how to present themselves in person at an interview. This is where your help can be most practical. With the information provided in Chapter 6 you will be able to advise in a confident manner and be sure that your knowledge is up to date and appropriate. Guidelines about dress and image are also included which may represent new ideas for some careers advisers, but are an increasingly important part of successful achievement in the current competitive employment market.

The concluding chapter draws together all the information provided and gives you a comprehensive checklist for giving good careers advice to your clients. Throughout all the chapters you will find a series of case studies of typical real-life careers problems which will illustrate the points made. Quotations from able and sensitive advisers with whom I have worked are added to provide different perspectives on the nature of the work.

Chapter 1

Career Choice

'One of the best ways to empower a client is to give them permission to have lots of different ideas about their future.'
Careers Officer working with 13–16 year olds

What is careers advice?

The Concise Oxford Dictionary defines 'career' as 'course or progress through life', which is a fairly wide explanation. It can therefore involve paid work, periods spent on domestic responsibilities, voluntary work, retirement activities and temporary and part-time employment. In fact, any activity can come into the definition, because at any one time it may be in an individual's interest to pursue one or more of these different options.

Careers advice is therefore about choosing the next best step in the course of one's life, with the understanding that our career may change direction, be put on hold for periods or perhaps take two steps back for each one forward. For most of us, sorting out our career is a difficult act to carry out and we find it helpful to be able to consult an expert. Careers advisers represent the experts. They are trained to offer independent and unbiased guidance to their clients. The main activity of careers work in this country is helping school and college students to choose a suitable career or occupation, but increasingly adults are also being offered guidance. Unemployed people can obtain help and counselling and people in employment can get advice if they want to change career.

The job of advising other people about their careers is quite a logical process. There is no mystery here. Advising about someone's career will involve getting to know clients in the following ways:

The past

- What have they done in the past?
- What skills have they acquired; what education and training have they had, whether full or part-time, formal or informal?
- What experience have they had, whether paid or unpaid, part-time or voluntary work?
- What responsibilities have they shouldered, and what have they achieved?
- Which career ideas have they explored previously?

The present

- In which activities are they currently involved?
- What are they doing to further their career plans presently?
- How do they spend their leisure time; what commitments do they have and how do they organise their life at the moment?
- How does their present role or job plan fit in with what might happen next?
- What problems are they currently having to deal with?

The future

- What are their hopes, dreams and plans for the future?
- What are they doing to move on in life?
- What events lie ahead and what responsibilities are they going to have in the foreseeable future?
- What problems or barriers might exist for them in the coming years and months?

Personality

- How would they describe themselves in terms of personality strengths, and would other people who know them agree with that description?
- What are they like in and out of the working environment?
- What excites and depresses them?
- How do they work with others, and alone?
- What would they like to change about themselves, and what would they, and others, describe as their greatest weaknesses?

Once all or some of these relevant questions have been asked, a guidance worker can begin to piece together an understanding of the client – rather like forming the pieces of a complicated jigsaw puzzle into a full picture. Of course, people are not neat puzzles and the guidance is perhaps more of a detective story, using the clues available to formulate options for progress.

How does careers guidance happen?

Many of us give advice in an informal way to people we know but in the same way that suggesting causes for a friend's stomach-ache does not make us a doctor, so well-meant career suggestions do not a careers adviser make! Formal careers guidance is most often provided by careers officers in schools and colleges and there is a statutory duty for such a facility to be available for those leaving full-time education. The service may be arranged by the local authority, local education authority in partnership with a local Training and Enterprise Council or Local Enterprise Company, or through a private company specifically funded for that purpose. Universities employ their own advisers to give careers advice to their students. In the future it is likely that privately run companies will play an increasing role in supplying this provision.

In addition, there are other people now involved in advising about career development such as companies or organisations who offer training courses; employers wishing to advise their staff; higher education colleges; those working with unemployed people and job seekers; school staff; enlightened trade unions wishing to provide an improved service to their members; or adult education advisers and lecturers. Certain organisations exist to give solely educational advice in particular – informing and explaining about which courses exist locally for which career.

Other organisations which may occasionally provide advice about careers as part of their work include the Probation Service, Youth Service and Employment Service, community centres and voluntary organisations which deal with people looking for work, and the professional associations and institutes catering for the different professions. Private enterprise is represented in careers guidance most usually in the form of guidance agencies who charge individuals and companies to advise their staff, and in the plethora of independent careers advisers who regularly advertise their services in local papers up and down the country. The huge market for magazines aimed mainly at women and all serious newspapers include regular items on career development and issues relating to the changing world of work.

Where does it occur?

When we are talking about the formal sector, most careers work takes the form of one-to-one interviews between a client and an adviser. The adviser can adopt many different names. I have heard of them calling themselves:

- Careers officers
- Careers advisers
- Careers counsellors
- Careers consultants
- Careers associates

- Careers guidance counsellors
- Vocational advisers
- Guidance counsellors

and there are bound to be many other variations on these themes. The permutations seem endless and are often an attempt to define precisely the way the job is performed and to differentiate the advisers from those of a different service nearby. People who specialise in advising at times of redundancy, themselves often employed by companies, might be called outplacement specialists or redundancy counsellors.

Because of the diversity of provision of careers advice, informal and basic guidance can be given anywhere, from a church environment to over a drink at the local pub. Careers advice conducted in groups can take place at any location where the service is offered in the same way as any group teaching or seminar would be offered. When the advice is given one to one the interview will normally take place either in an educational setting such as a school or a college, at an employer's premises or at those of the providing organisation. Advisers would normally occupy a small interview room for this purpose which is private, or at least where clients can talk easily, without the worry of being overheard, and which is as comfortable as possible, while also providing a purposeful setting in which to discuss the issues and make wise choices.

What does an adviser do?

There are nearly as many variations in the types of work done, as in the job titles available but there are some key activities which we can discuss. Those readers new to the field may be surprised at the variety in the work:

- Providing information about different types of work or training
- Talking through an individual client's career ideas and aspirations

- Researching the different options available on behalf of a client
- Working with groups of clients to explore career directions or to give job-search help
- Giving presentations and writing reports on careers issues
- Giving tests or questionnaires to ascertain abilities or career ideas for clients
- Acting as a referral service to education or training providers or to employers
- Acting as an advocate to represent a client to another organisation
- Giving advice on labour markets and recruitment practice to employers.

Full-time careers advisers working in different environments and organisations will stress different parts of the job according to the priorities of the organisation for which they work. There are other activities which could be added to the list above which may be carried out by certain advisers at particular times according to the needs of the job. Some people see the work being much more concerned with conveying accurate information about different careers, and see less significance in protracted sessions of 'just talk'. Others will find that the liaison activity is more important where they work, so visiting local employers and training organisations will be more prevalent. More important than any one single activity in the work, an adviser has to be able to strike up a businesslike but supportive relationship with the client.

What training is needed?

A wide variety of subjects can be studied to enable a student to feel well-trained as a careers counsellor and these will be covered in more detail in Chapter 3, on the role of the adviser. The main areas include:

- Helping skills.

- Establishing and agreeing the purpose of the interview or group work.
- Exploring the situation – involving assessment, focusing, attending, empathy, respect, genuineness, concreteness and questioning. Contract building. Establishing relationships.
- Understanding the issues or goal setting – involving giving and sharing of information and clarifying goals. Giving and taking feedback. Being open and encouraging concrete ideas and suggestions.
- Formulating an action plan – involving generating ideas, planning, choosing between alternatives and helping to set specific targets for action.
- Putting the plan into effect and evaluating the result – involving motivating, rewarding and supporting.

There is a growing range of ways to train in this field. There are full-time and part-time courses, but opportunities for distance learning are limited. The mushrooming of Accreditation of Prior Learning (APL) may offer new careers workers a way to get credit for experience already gained towards a guidance qualification. The Local Government Management Board (address on page 111 provides details of current courses available leading to the Diploma in Careers Guidance. This course, which concentrates on work with school-age students, is still the most common course at post-graduate level but increasingly the wider-focused Vocational Guidance Diploma, which offers modules to learn about work with a more adult client group, is being introduced. Some people get a rarer qualification in educational guidance, specifically related to helping clients with choices about courses and training.

Lower level courses exist in general counselling which can provide a useful introduction to the interpersonal skills needed and the techniques of the helping interview. Introductory short counselling courses can offer a few days or weeks of discussion and practice of the issues involved in the work. While not representing a full or thorough training, for those who work on the support side of the guidance process, perhaps as administrators or clerical staff, such courses give a valuable understanding of the role of the facilitator and ways to work with people in a counselling setting.

What makes a good adviser?

Chapter 3 looks into the role of the careers adviser in more detail. It is a good question whether careers advisers are born or made. I believe that people can be trained in the practical skills necessary, such as:

- researching information
- interview techniques, including methods of questioning
- handling groups of young people or adults
- creating action plans as focused targets in written form
- organising their work and managing their time
- working as part of a team.

However, few jobs involved with other people rely on practical effectiveness alone. To make a difference to a client the adviser needs to have a natural affinity with other people. This involves curiosity about the world of work, the ability to see matters from another's point of view (empathy) and the detachment to avoid judging others by your own standards. It means that the adviser needs to enjoy talking to others and must be able to keep his or her own wishes and priorities out of the frame and concentrate instead on putting the clients' interests to the fore. This requires an essential selflessness (altruism), thoughtfulness about other people's needs and the ability to be aware of one's own feelings and prejudices. These qualities are not easy to teach unless they already exist in some measure, although they can be encouraged.

Advisers should be interested in others generally and be good at finding out a lot about other people without too much difficulty, but without being nosy just for its own sake. To work all week with needy people requires a sense of humour, considerable stamina and the ability to switch off from other people's problems at the end of each day. Careers counsellors need to be able to take the long view and feel good about their work even though they may rarely be able to see the results of it themselves. I firmly believe that it is essential to have had experience of the world of work before presuming to advise other people on how to enter, survive and make a success of it.

Some people would argue that the particular style in which you interact with clients matters less than the ability to be very patient, friendly, capable of inspiring trust in others and able to get people to talk to you. It helps to have a sense of purpose and to be able to focus on outcomes. You also need to convey to clients, particularly young people, what has happened to them during the course of their careers advice.

Some of the best careers advisers I have known have also been creative people. I do not mean that they were necessarily trained artists, but that they had imaginative ways of communicating with clients. Rather than take notes during an interview in the typical manner, they would draw pictures, arrows and symbols to represent the client's words. If this is done with coloured pens on a large sheet of white paper, it is often the case that the client feels particularly involved with the process and wants to keep it as a record afterwards.

Steve had come to see the adviser asking for information about nursing. He seemed in a hurry and not keen to talk. Abi, the adviser, said it would be easy to give him the information he wanted but asked if she could have a brief chat to him first. Once she started asking him a bit more about his interest in nursing, where it had originated and how much he knew about the subject, Steve opened up.

It turned out that his father was involved in the medical profession and had wanted him to follow a similar career. Steve himself was not convinced by the idea but had not made any other career plans. He was only trying to keep his family off his back by visiting the adviser.

After a constructive enquiry into his interests and abilities,

Steve left the office with plenty of material for him to consider and discuss with his family. He felt very stimulated by the ideas generated in the session and made another appointment in two weeks to take the process further.

How are career decisions made?

Since the first client received advice from the first adviser, there have been attempts to describe the significant factors present in career development in order to shed light on any patterns of behaviour or requirements which may exist. Theoretical models can be a constructive guide to what often occurs, delineating parameters to help frame and inform the role of the adviser. The disadvantages of such schools of thought include the possibility of ignoring factors which do not fit with the theory and being too restrictive or prescriptive about the way guidance should be offered. Established theories can deny new ideas their true impact and create the impression that there are rigidly right and wrong ways to practice.

There are various established traditions of thought, or models of guidance.

Theories which stress the significance of *psychological factors* suggest that the characteristics of people, including their interests, aptitudes and personality, determine the career which best suits them. Therefore the number of choices available to an individual is only limited by that person's own traits and abilities. The development of personality and aptitude tests provides the diagnostic tools of this school of thought and it is considered worth while to spend time finding out about different jobs in order to see where the best match with an individual client will take place.

Sociological models, on the other hand, suggest that the environment in which an individual finds him or herself will be the main determinant of life choices available. At its most extreme, this school of thought would say that much careers input will be of only marginal use because factors such as social class, educational opportunity, income and area of residence will effectively act as a constraint on free career choice.

Developmental theory says that career choice is a developing factor with most people and is therefore a life-long process. As people live and learn, they will include and exclude different options in their portfolio and will change their choices at each new stage of their lives. The fantasy stage of the young teenager will give way to the experimental stage, the consolidating stage and so on. This school of thought implies that school-age choices will be short lived and that perhaps the most effective careers guidance should be available throughout life rather than being concentrated in the educational sector.

I label *contingency theory* as that which represents an amalgam and a development of all the above, thinking that parts of each apply. Those advisers who do not feel comfortable interpreting clients' experiences in the light of any one particular school of thought will pick out the best of each to describe more precisely the process which is taking place. They agree that societal elements have an influence on career choice, but would argue that they are not the only significant factors, or no one would ever go to university unless their parents had, for example. It is true that we all go through different life stages, but not all 35-year-olds want the same type of life experience as each other. It is true that we have differing aptitudes and abilities, but we can learn and change according to our motivation and urge to do so.

Chapter 2

The Client

'You never know who will walk in through the door next, or what they will want to discuss.' College careers counsellor

Who wants careers advice?

At different times in their lives anyone can feel the need for careers advice and it is often as a response to some critical event. Unemployment or redundancy can prompt a person to want to think about his or her next step. In a recession many people, although still working, are under-employed because they are in jobs which offer little or no long-term satisfaction. They dare not leave because they know that finding a better alternative could be very difficult.

Vicky was unemployed for the first time in her life after a period of self-employment. Her confidence was very low after the failure of her business and she did not really know what to do next. She managed to get an appointment with Paul, the adviser, and said that she wanted to talk through her ideas.

As a result of their session, Vicky realised that the recession was partly to blame for her bad luck in the business and that she had acquired a lot of skills during the last three years. With Paul's guidance she put together a list of possible next steps to research in the careers section of her local library.

What sort of help do they need?

These are some of the subjects about which people approach careers advisers:

- Information about the possibilities
- Pointers to the future of a particular area of work
- Referral to a particular scheme, course or employer
- Tips on presenting themselves in person and in writing
- Guidelines on what action to take and when
- To check out that they are on the right lines and are taking a sensible approach
- To get help to see what they might like to do
- Encouragement to keep on trying
- Motivation to burst through barriers
- The confidence to aim high and to succeed
- To answer the question 'Where am I going in my life?'

Rodney was of Afro-Caribbean descent, aged 21, unemployed and thoroughly depressed and cynical about his employment prospects. He had never had a proper job and was convinced that there was no point in trying because of the racial discrimination he believed he would face in any recruitment process.

He had three guidance interviews with his careers officer, Karon, before finally agreeing to join a training programme. He was suspicious that it would lead nowhere but could appreciate that the longer he was unemployed the less chance there would be of any employer being interested in him.

Karon was able to recommend a scheme that she knew from experience would involve a life-skills element to boost Rodney's confidence. During his 12 months he kept in contact with the careers office, and once Karon managed to persuade his manager not to throw him out after Rodney had been through a particularly rocky patch.

Eighteen months later, he is still not employed but is working on a voluntary basis with the scheme where he trained and is coaching a local basketball team. He is determined to keep applying for jobs and has got a place on an access course which is designed to lead on to higher education, next September.

How does the client feel?

Most people feel a bit scared and can feel very vulnerable when they have to ask for help. Any expert, however friendly, can appear intimidating – merely sitting at the doctor's surgery is a fairly daunting experience. Even if the matter in question is not deeply personal and private, it is slightly demeaning to admit that you do not already know all the answers about your life. This is particularly true of some adults who feel that being grown up means that they should know exactly where they are going and what they hope to achieve.

At the other age of the spectrum, young people are more used to consulting adults, but some young men find it acutely uncomfortable to have to talk to another person about what they want from their career. The reward for pushing through these barriers of embarrassment and awkwardness is that for some men and particularly younger school-age males, this kind of interaction can make the difference to their ability to see where to go next. For many this will be the first time they have shared such thoughts with another person, and have been taken seriously. Such an experience can change lives.

Julie could see that Sue was very nervous as they started their appointment at the adult guidance centre. The adviser decided to call on her knowledge of body language. She deliberately and unobtrusively altered her sitting position so that her body shape directly mirrored that of her client. She put her head slightly to one side to exaggerate her listening pose and stopped taking notes in order to better attend to Sue. Smiling to encourage her, she opened her eyes more widely, and nodded to show that she was interested in everything Sue was saying. She unclasped her hands to make her posture open and accessible and concentrated on keeping extra still and quiet.

When Julie later read the customer feedback sheet that Sue had completed this is what she found:

'I am a shy person and normally hate opening up about myself in front of strangers, but the adviser I saw was easy to talk to and I found the experience very constructive and helpful. Thank you.'

Julie had used all the skills she knew in order to relate well to Sue.

What rights does the client have?

Respectful treatment

Tom was at his wits end to know what to do with his latest client, Sarah. She was barely civil, seemed to have a massive chip on her shoulder and her answers suggested that she felt the world owed her a living. After half an hour of getting nowhere fast, at last he decided to back a hunch:

'Being unemployed leaves scars, doesn't it?' he tried. Sarah was quiet for a moment and he wondered if he had completely misjudged the situation.

She replied in a small voice:

'I feel I'm not worth much to anyone any more. I wouldn't even employ me now if I was an employer. What am I going to do?'

Once Tom had got through to the demoralised and depressed Sarah who was hiding behind an aggressive exterior it was easier to work together on some small but constructive steps forward. A local job search course put her in touch with others in her situation. Realising that she was not alone increased her confidence by leaps and bounds and she began to see that unemployment was causing her feelings. With help she established a purposeful and determined job search programme for herself and she has recently received a job offer.

It may sound a trifle dramatic to recommend having a box of paper tissues to hand at all times, but it is one way of minimising the distress caused to those rare cases who get upset in your presence.

Confidentiality

Don't just make this a claim on a publicity leaflet. Ensure that the things that are shared in your careers guidance sessions really are kept private within your service. Be wary of talking about clients to your colleagues in an open plan office too. Even if you do not mention any names, any waiting clients who happen to hear you will imagine that you will be laughing at them as soon as they are out of earshot. It is a valid part of learning on the job to discuss specific examples of career problems with colleagues to share methods of treatment and ideas for helping the clients, but always retain respect for the individuals concerned in any case being aired.

How do you attract more clients?

The obvious answer is 'by providing what the clients want'. This needs to be done and it also needs to be *seen* to be done.

Manner

You need to put clients at their ease as quickly as possible. A smile goes a long way to reassure visitors that you mean them no harm. It may seem ridiculous to say that clients would be fearful of their careers adviser, but subconsciously we are all slightly afraid of a stranger with whom we are committed to sharing our thoughts and feelings. Clients need to be made to feel comfortable and relaxed in order to talk and think freely. Do not forget to introduce yourself clearly, and it also makes good sense to greet visitors with a handshake too, to show respect and a business-like attitude. Even if you do not normally operate this way, I recommend trying to cultivate the habit. Initial friendly small-talk can establish the right relationship early on and get the client talking freely before more serious subjects need to be raised. Remember that what seems obvious to you may be very confusing for a new client. The fact that you may take some notes to help you remember the main points of the interview should be clearly explained so that your client does not worry about what he or she has said to make you write a comment down.

Environment

It is important to make sure that visitors to your organisation or office feel that they are going to have a good experience. The physical aspects of the setting in which clients are seen can have a major impact on the way that they view the whole experience. Think how different it feels to attend an interview in an old-style benefit office compared to an appointment in a modern employment agency. Of course, the amount you can do with your environment will depend on the resources available and the space which can be used. As an image consultant I am keen that the appearance of each encounter is seen as important. The point at which clients arrive is key to the impression they receive about their forthcoming experience with you. Fresh flowers are always a positive, welcoming touch in a reception or careers area.

Modern retailing practice dictates that shops have large plate glass windows in order that the customers can see inside the shop, recognise their escape route, and therefore feel that it is safe to go inside. One problem of any careers advice, like any counselling work, is that it is largely unseen by the general public and therefore something of a mystery. The safer you can make the situation seem, the better – and the less time it will take to make your client feel relaxed when you meet. If you are ever thanked for your help by a grateful client, ask them to put their gratitude in writing and then frame the resulting letter on the wall. Your next clients can read how helpful your service was when they are waiting to see you. They will arrive for their interview in an expectant and encouraged mood.

A warm but not stifling temperature, comfortable but not easy chairs, and a surface to write on will be needed. Some interviewers prefer to use a small coffee table to increase the informality, whereas others find it too difficult to write or take computer notes without a proper desk. If you are one of the increasing number of advisers who take a computerised record during the interview, or even with note-taking, make sure that you are making the process as accessible as possible to the client. If you choose to have a desk top between you and your subject, ensure that you are both seated across the corner if at all possible. Facing each other on opposite sides of a desk only leads to a very formal and distant feeling for the client, hardly the desired ambience!

Most careers advisers think that the more privacy that you can create, the better. Interestingly, the research that I have seen shows that clients are less worried about complete privacy as long as they feel that the interviewer is attending to them and that they are not distracted by telephones or other people. Indeed, for some of our more nervous clients it can be more intimidating to be taken away to a remote interviewing room than it would be to sit slightly apart from a busy reception or library area.

What puts clients off?

Clients are in a vulnerable position when asking for your guidance. Comments which you feel will be helpful, which are delivered in a direct and definite way, can sometimes be perceived in a quite different light by your clients. Criticism too early in the relationship between you and your clients which is not delivered in a constructive way alienates people. Clients respond to advisers who are obviously putting themselves out for other people and no client minds an adviser who does not have all the answers as long as he or she admits it openly and does not try to cover up this ignorance with bluff.

Some clients feel disappointed after careers advice because they do not feel that they have been told the answer to their career problems. There is rarely one simple solution anyway, and sometimes none, so it needs to be carefully and clearly explained to clients what you can offer and what you cannot at the outset of any guidance work. Keep promises that you make to clients or do not make them. If it is unlikely that you can get careers information back to a client within one week, let them know the truth. Otherwise you will both waste your time, the client waiting for the documents and you feeling horribly guilty!

Another off-putting experience is the adviser who rules out options incorrectly. You may feel sure that there is no free, full-time training in horticulture available in your area, for instance, but beware of being too definite about local opportunities without a full check, as new courses could have started or new funding arrangements been established since you last researched the subject.

Some school-age clients can be put off the whole idea of careers advice because they are obliged to attend a compulsory guidance interview in their final year with someone that they have never met before. Guidance given when it is not required will not be wanted. The best that advisers can do in this circumstance is at least try to make the whole experience as positive as possible. That way the young person concerned can come back, perhaps down to the careers office, at a later stage when they really could benefit from some help from that adviser they met once in school who seemed 'all right'.

The available evidence suggests that the best way to introduce guidance in any setting is to introduce the subject to the client as early as you can in as many and varied ways as possible, giving as much information about the benefits of guidance as can be conveyed in the time available. In a school setting, this may involve being seen around the school, going into class groups to introduce yourself, appearing at parents' evenings and providing careers 'drop in' sessions in advance of the planned interview programme. In a careers centre for adults, the more evidence you can provide in the reception area of the success stories credited to the centre, the more your new clients will want to partake of the services offered.

Chapter 3

The Role of the Adviser

'Do not underestimate the impression that you can make on a client. You are invested with a great deal of automatic authority as an adviser even if you feel uncertain of your position yourself.' Careers officer working with school leavers

Let us first consider the crux of the adviser's role and examine the difference between the various terms used for giving help with career choice. In this book I have used the terms 'advice', 'guidance' and 'counselling' almost interchangeably. In the Concise Oxford Dictionary they are all defined in a very similar way.

Advice: this refers to 'opinion given or offered as to action, information given'. Often advice starts with the words 'You should ...'

Guidance: 'acting as a guide to, leading, directing course of action'. Often guidance starts with the words 'You could ...'

Counselling: 'giving advice to' but may involve a more in-depth analysis of a client's history, aspirations and personality. The result of a counselling interaction may be that the options would be laid out for the client to decide for him or herself which to choose.

An old joke in careers circles is that if you as a client want to know the correct time, someone giving advice would say: 'The time is three o'clock'; someone giving guidance would say: 'There's the clock, let's look at it together and you can tell me what time you think it is'; and a counsellor would take you by the hand, lead you up to the clock and ask: 'How do you feel about this clock and what time you would like it to be?'

Different styles of giving guidance

Advisers can adopt different relationships with their clients according to the demands of the helping situation and their own personalities and preferred method of connecting with other people.

That of *friend* may be appropriate where the main need is to listen and respond to a client. Overt advice is not always either wanted or needed, but an adviser who can help a client in a dispassionate and sympathetic manner to see the available options without taking sides can be a real asset.

That of quasi *parent* can be a possibility in some circumstances where a client needs gentle guidance in the form of suggested outcomes coupled with a positive regard and ongoing support. The adviser here may give direct encouragement and motivation to enable the client to move forward.

Less often, a role more like that of a *teacher* will be needed where the client is led to discover the most appropriate answer, through an evaluation of the evidence available or when the adviser is making presentations to groups of clients. The 'teacher' adviser may feel that a client needs to have high expectations set in order for them to achieve their chosen career development.

Sometimes you will need to act like a traditional *counsellor*, letting your clients talk through their experiences to help them find their way through the current problem. Sometimes this will involve the adviser hardly talking at all, particularly with the more articulate, older clients. Here it is helpful if you can virtually merge into the surroundings and let your own personality go unnoticed so that clients have an almost therapeutic experience, learning and listening to their own thought processes made audible through you.

For some factual points of information you can take on more of an *authority* role. For instance, if you are advising a young man about training to be an electrician and you discover that he is colour blind, you can immediately say with full confidence that there is no way that he would ever be accepted on to such a course. There are no exceptions to this rule and although your client may be desperate for such a qualification, he needs to understand why it would not be possible and then be helped to select other options.

The idea of being a *role-model* can seem an odd part to suggest, but for a lot of clients meeting someone who takes their career development seriously can sanction the whole idea of investing time and trouble in themselves.

For most advisers there will be times when all these different roles, or versions of them, are required. Most important is the imperative to be flexible, try to anticipate clients' needs and to respond in an appropriate way. You do not need to feel that you should have all the answers. If in doubt about the best guidance to give a client, it may be helpful to express that by outlining the different options available and encouraging the client to state the advantages and disadvantages of each. A summary of the position will often make the situation clearer and provoke further discussion which can lead to a satisfactory conclusion.

Helping skills

There are many books on counselling techniques which explain the key terms in great detail. The current and predominant thought in careers counselling is based on Gerard Egan's book, *The Skilled Helper* (Brooks Cole Publishing Company, California, 1990), which created a system of stages of work with a client. It is not aimed specifically at vocational counselling, but the process is essentially the same, even if the depth of interaction may be less than in some other counselling situations.

The main skills that an adviser needs in order to relate well to clients are as follows:

Looking and acting the part

Careers advisers need to look convincing as people who are knowledgeable and successful (remember the role-model aspect of your work). Clients respond to the same signals as you do. While you do not want to appear like a ruthless corporate executive, you should ensure that your clothes are neat and appropriate. By appropriate, I mean not distracting or too casual. You are setting yourself up as an expert on the world of work and training. You need to look as though you can handle your own career properly before any client will allow you to have an influence over theirs.

Some people involved in work with the public think that to look smart will alienate their clients. This is a fallacy. In fact the research which has been undertaken suggests that clients tend to be more impressed by someone who looks competent and well organised. They always prefer to talk to someone who appears together and business-like than to someone who appears rumpled and messy.

Follow these guidelines:

- Dress simply but smartly, with nothing too tight or short.
- Do not overdo your make-up or accessories.
- Save jewellery for after work. Do not wear dangly earrings or distinctive badges which may distract your audience.
- Plain, neutral colours and a comfortable cut of clothes are best for work.
- Spend as much money on clothes as you can afford and get the best quality available within your price range.
- It is better to dress up than dress down. If in doubt, dress one grade higher than your own job and you cannot go wrong.
- Make sure that your paperwork and other necessary paraphernalia are prepared before you see a client – do not create a bad first impression by faffing around with bits of paper when you could be talking.
- Keep any messes out of sight and your desk clear, so that no distractions detract from your purpose.

- Make sure that colleagues know that you are seeing someone and are only to be disturbed by the phone or in person in an emergency.
- However much is going on in your work or private life, allow your clients full access to an uncluttered brain; you will need to give complete concentration to the task in hand.

Establishing relationships

When you first meet a client you need to be able to establish rapport and a feeling of comfort. A relaxed posture and a friendly smile can help your client to feel secure in your company. You need to come over as somebody with confidence in your abilities, who is authoritative but not intimidating. Good careers counselling relies on your having the confidence to be accessible to your clients and giving them as much control over your relationship as possible.

Do explain to anyone you are seeing what you are planning to do. If you want them to follow you to a private interview room I suggest:

'Would you like to come with me? We can go to a room just down the corridor where we can have more of a chat.'

This may seem very basic advice but at this point in your encounter your clients will be at their most anxious about what they have let themselves in for. For all they know you are a lunatic whose sole aim is to belittle their hard-earned experience and ridicule their career plans. Their first impression of you can be crucial to the way that your relationship develops. If you can come across as pleasant and open, they will respond. If you have had a bad day or are hung over from the night before, you may well have to act a part here in order not to let your discomfort or tetchiness show.

Contract building

'Contract' is a term used in counselling circles. It is applied in a slightly different way to its legal meaning. Establishing a contract can be likened to setting the agenda for your meeting. Like an agenda, it should be agreed in advance by the parties involved. Unlike a formal agenda, it is a verbal agreement rather than a written one. It should lay down the broad outline of what will happen during the interview. Good examples of early questions to help you formulate your contract could be:

'Tell me a bit about what brings you here.'

'How can I help you today?'

'Perhaps you would like to start by telling me about what you hope to get from this interview.'

Once your client has explained their initial enquiry or problem, it should be possible for you to frame a plan which you can then put to them for their agreement, for example:

'So you are interested in legal work. Suppose we spend some time finding out about you and where that idea comes from, and then I can tell you more about the sorts of work and training available.'

'You feel that you have reached a cross-roads in your career. Some friends have suggested re-training and you would like to check that idea out as well as considering if anything else is appropriate.'

'It sounds as though you would like some help with your job search activities and to brush up on your interview technique.'

These three statements are examples of contract setting. No one can say what will be appropriate in advance as it depends on what the client wants to talk about when you meet. What is needed from you here is the ability to listen attentively to what the client is saying, pick up any clues from the particular words that he or she is using and summarise the points they have made.

Do not be tempted to feel that you are taking all the responsibility for this part of the interview. You can trust the clients to participate in this process. Say to them:

'Does that sound the sort of thing you expected?' or

'Is that the way you would like to spend this time?' or

'What do you think of that plan for our time today?'

They will then feel able to tell you if they were expecting to get something else from you.

Exploring the situation

This is the next step of the adviser's job and it involves attending closely to what the client is saying and showing through body language and facial expression. It can be hard work and often quite exhausting if you have to see too many clients one after the other. If your client has crossed arms and legs, is wearing a deep frown and is trying to move her chair as far away from you as possible, you may wonder if there is something wrong. Do not just wonder in silence – check it out. Tell her that you get the impression that she may be feeling a bit uncomfortable and see if she wishes to identify any problem that you can sort out together.

Empathy is a term which means being able to put yourself in your client's position to understand his or her career problem. To get close to someone whom you have not met before in a short space of time you need to show respect, and be genuine in your interest in what they are saying. Your aim must be to try and firm up the themes which your client brings up, helping him or her to focus. Try wherever possible not to direct your clients to answer questions in a particular way by the way you phrase the question.

'How do you think this is going so far?' will probably get you a more honest answer than 'This seems to be going well so far, don't you think?', which makes it very difficult for the client to answer in the negative.

Giving and taking feedback

Careers guidance is not just about getting people to like you or to talk freely to you. It has got to get somewhere as a result

– at least to a new understanding and plan of action. Part of the art of helping people to come to decisions about their future is aided by giving them feedback on their own thoughts and words. Although it seems a straightforward thing to tell people what they seem to have just said to you, it can prove very helpful. We all can find it difficult to see the wood for the trees at times, and having someone sum up their impressions of what we have been saying can shed light on previously hidden feelings.

'You seem to be particularly attached to your colleagues at work. Perhaps you do not feel quite ready to leave there yet?'

'You have twice mentioned your regret at not going to college after school. Shall we talk about that time in a bit more detail?

The other side of giving feedback of course, is receiving it. If you ask questions, have hunches and put suggestions to your clients, they may well disagree with you, or not be happy with the way that the interview is going. This should not appear as a problem, for as long as you have been consulting them as you go along, you can always try changing tack altogether to the satisfaction of you both.

Understanding the issues and goal setting

This involves the giving and sharing of information, and then clarifying goals. To some extent understanding the issues comes from experience, but it is also helped by being able to get inside the head of your client and to ask them the trigger questions which allow them to make connections and see things in perspective again. A good counsellor will share information when appropriate, for example younger clients are often reassured by knowing you found career choice difficult yourself. I often joke with clients that careers advisers spend their lives trying to decide what they are going to be when they grow up.

To set any goals you need to recognise where you have got to. At some point you need to move beyond sharing information and finding out all about your client in order to give the event some purpose. This can involve a jump to a new position in discussion terms. You need to develop the interview and it is often a good idea to express that need openly:

'Well, we have talked a fair bit about your interests and past experience. Let us now see if we can tie all this together and work out how to take your plans forwards.'

might be one way of tackling it. Sometimes this more direct comment might do the trick:

'I am conscious of the time moving on. Perhaps we need to take stock at this point and see where we are getting to.'

These kinds of statement can help you both to focus on what is going to happen as a result of the interview.

Formulating an action plan

This can involve generating ideas with, or sometimes for, your client. Do not worry if no concrete outcome has developed from the interview. In this case the client probably needs to spend time doing some reading about different options or thinking a bit more about themselves. A good plan will be enthusiastically taken up by the client. If he or she looks doubtful, or sounds hesitant about this stage of the discussion, ask him or her to comment on what has happened so far.

Choosing between alternatives should come from the client and not from the adviser, although it is perfectly acceptable for you to suggest priorities. Setting specific targets for action is the last stage of the careers guidance process and needs complete agreement from the client for the targets to be met. Get him to propose the time scale and build in flexibility in case the plan does not work out. If selecting one option is proving impossible, that probably means that there is no one best choice and it may be more productive for the client to proceed with several options in parallel, and gather more information until one option becomes the most attractive.

Do not be tempted to undertake lots of work yourself on the clients' behalf. Getting a job or course requires determination, and spoon-feeding a client by making appointments for interviews and filling in forms for them only lets them off the first hook and denies them the achievement of taking their own first steps to a rewarding career. The difficulties are all part of the chosen journey, and the sooner your client learns that, the better.

Putting the plan into effect

The need to motivate clients is one of the most important tasks for you. Apart from feeling awkward about having to ask for your help in the first place, finding a path to follow rather than just sitting and waiting can be hard work. Give freely of your encouragement and support for sensible plans and realistic targets. The rewards you can offer are your continued interest and admiration for their efforts in getting to wherever they want to get to.

Conducting group work

Teaching careers or job-search help to groups is a slightly different type of work. Here, the responsibility is on you for keeping the discussion going and covering the important aspects. You will need to be reassuring and up-beat and encouraging. The more positive you can be with group members, while sticking to your work plan for the session, the more they will contribute and learn.

In most cases, unless it is to be a completely unstructured discussion group, you will need to plan your work thoroughly in advance. You need to practise talking in public as often as possible to get rid of your nerves, which, in any case, will not show nearly as much as you think. A short course on the basics of public speaking can pay dividends for most people in terms of confidence in making presentations. Be aware that your own appearance and body language can influence the progress of a session. Experiment with the physical environment too by having different chair and table arrangements for the repeated sessions. A horseshoe-shaped line of chairs provokes a much more intimate and involved group than rows of chairs and tables.

As an adviser you need to understand from your own experience what makes for effective and ineffective counselling behaviour. You need to pinpoint what constitutes being helpful, and develop a set of basic skills that can be applied to careers problems. The factors which work in careers guidance are in essence those same points which work in any helping context, although it is important to realise the difference between giving careers advice and other counselling work. Careers advisers are only interested in finding out about their clients in order to help them move or develop towards their expressed career aims in some way – which does not mean that in every case there will be some change of circumstances as the outcome.

Consider Pippa's case:

Pippa works as a trainee accountant for a small firm of chartered accountants and is two-thirds of the way through her training. Although she loves her work, she is not happy with the company because of a personality clash between herself and someone in her section. She is also feeling frustrated because the supervisors do not seem interested in helping to sort out the resulting bad atmosphere. Pippa talked the problem through with a careers adviser. She expressed the resentment she felt, and explored the options open to her:

- Leaving and trying to find another company with which to continue her training
- Giving up accountancy altogether and changing career direction
- Staying where she is until her training period is completed.

Having considered the alternatives fully during her careers guidance interview, she decided, after weighing up the pros and cons of each option, that she would stay where she was until her training was finished. She would take no action as a result of the interview but would try to keep out of the way of her troublesome colleague as much as possible. Although Pippa was not going to make any career move, she said after the interview:

'I just needed someone to talk to, to check that I wasn't making a mistake by staying where I am. As soon as we looked at the different choices available, I realised that it would be in my best interests to stay put until I am qualified and then move to a better-managed company.'

If we assume that all clients attend voluntarily, choosing to avail themselves of careers help, then it can be seen that not every careers intervention will result in change. But every careers intervention should be of help to the client.

In the next example, the adviser felt unable to help properly:

The interview with Rob was not going well. He had seemed unhappy and agitated since the beginning and talked at some length about his medical problems. He had been extensively treated for depression and was currently under medication. Although he said he felt better than he used to, he had left his last job a year ago because of his ill health, had been on sickness benefit ever since and repeated that he was not interested in work or training yet.

Harriet, the careers counsellor, took a deep breath, and decided to express what was on her mind.

'It doesn't seem as though you are ready for the move back into the employment market yet,' she said. 'It sounds as though you could take your time about that decision and take the time to work out exactly where you want to go next. I think you will need the help of a medical counsellor before you will feel ready to come here.'

She referred him to a local mental health project where the workers had experience of Rob's situation and had access to the specialised help that Rob needed.

How does the adviser feel?

Everyone who is involved in any of the helping professions has to acknowledge their own needs, hopes and fears. I have never met a careers adviser who did not want to be liked and respected by his or her clients. It is a normal desire but the best advisers know that this will not always be the case if it is necessary for them to pass on information which their clients do not want to hear.

Some years back the government of the day launched the Youth Training Scheme with a prime time national advertising campaign on television. Featured prominently was a clip of a young man on a football scheme being picked out for stardom by the then manager of the England squad. Predictably, careers officers everywhere were deluged with enquiries from budding Ian Wrights and Gary Linekers. As there was only one very small football training scheme in existence anywhere at that time, careers advisers around the country were having to convey the bad news to their hopeful clients that it was highly unlikely they would even get a sniff at it.

One thing to remember is that we all feel scared when we think that our abilities will be tested. Your skills are those of listening, guiding and giving information, reflecting and helping the client to focus and be concrete about any resulting plans. Take a deep breath and follow these guidelines.

Do not panic

- When the client says, 'I don't know where I am going with my life!'. Although this seems daunting, you will be able to help him or her take this problem in small steps. You may need to book follow-up appointments to be truly helpful here, although a phrase like this is often just an expression of feelings of hopelessness. You will probably find that only one or more of the jigsaw pieces might be missing, and you will not be expected to give this client's life meaning.
- If the client stops talking. Pauses are often time for reflection and can add to the experience. Give your client time to follow his or her thoughts.
- If the client gets upset. Tears or anger mean that the discussion has just touched a raw nerve and it is unlikely

to be you who is causing the distress. Sometimes, if your clients are carrying a lot of guilt or deep emotion, they may even find it helpful to express it in this 'safe' forum.

- If you are getting confused or feel that the discussion is not getting anywhere. You cannot go wrong by expressing how you feel, and it is not your responsibility always to have the right answer. Some careers interviews end up with an agreement just to leave things alone for a while before another appointment might be made, because neither adviser nor client feels that it is proceeding particularly well.

What rights does the adviser have?

The right not to give guidance

In this age of under-resourced community care, services which are open to the general public will attract a certain number of clients with severe problems or disruptive behaviour. It does not help the client to provide time to discuss career development if he or she is obviously not ready or not able to consider the subject. Whether you are advising in a careers office, in a school or in a high street setting, you must feel free to recommend the client elsewhere or to terminate the interview or session if the problems presented need help other than your own.

The right to be safe

You must learn to trust your instincts about clients as it has been known for advisers to get hurt by disturbed clients during their work. If, for whatever reason, you feel that there is a danger from a particular person, act on your feelings and either defer the interview, conduct it in front of other people or make the client believe that there are several other people within calling distance.

The right to be treated with respect

You will find that there are some less mature clients who are resistant to the whole idea of career development. How they get to be sitting in front of a careers adviser, ostensibly for guidance, when they are obviously not taking the experience seriously is often down to coercion by whoever referred them to you in the first place. Whether they have come on threat of removal of benefit, or from their class tutor at his or her wits' end, it is best to express how you feel and then terminate the encounter if you are sure that it is just wasting the time of all concerned. The best advice and guidance in the world will be completely useless if the person to whom it is directed is not interested in hearing the message. Besides, you would not be in a position to interact fully with someone who resents being with you and who gives flippant, hostile or nonsensical answers to your questions.

The right not to have to see too many clients

My personal limit with adults whom I have not met before and who want careers advice of quite a complicated nature is six people in a day for one hour each. Any more appointments than that and I go home completely punch-drunk from the effort. Make sure that your work is as effective with the last client of the day as it was with the first, otherwise you may have to reduce the amount of time spent with each one, and book more repeat appointments.

What responsibilities does the adviser have?

Care

It is a great responsibility looking after other people. With careers guidance, we are often given only the most fleeting of interactions, say a 20-minute school talk or an hour-long interview, but unthinking comments or perceived criticisms can do untold damage. It is not part of your job to make clients feel bad, however unrealistic their ideas, but if you feel the need to carefully challenge their assumptions or beliefs, then you must explain fully why you are doing so. Make it perfectly clear that your opinions are not necessarily correct but are based on your experience and understanding, and then allow them to decide how they feel about your advice.

Confidentiality

When you promise confidentiality to someone, you must ensure that you mean what you say. Apart from the requirements of the Data Protection Act, which lays down standards for the information that you are allowed to keep on other people and the uses to which it may be put, you need to ensure that your records are kept private. It may seem harmless to discuss a client with friends or family but you must ensure that you do not give away any identifying clues about anybody or risk losing your reputation as a conscientious professional.

Objectivity

While the human being who has no biases or personal preferences has yet to be born, you need to acknowledge your prejudices and try to keep them out of the frame in your dealings with clients. Whether you are old, young, black, white, male, female, able-bodied or disabled, you need to be aware that you may make assumptions about clients and their abilities. Sometimes you will need to challenge the comments made by the clients themselves if they seem to be running themselves or other people down or setting their expectations too low.

A careers officer in school, Yvonne was interviewing Cherie, a fifth-year pupil. Cherie has had a steady boyfriend for a long time and was planning to get married in a couple of years' time. She said she would leave school as soon as possible but was not bothered about getting a job. She would just fill in the time until they could get a flat together. She wanted to have a baby, like her elder sister.

Yvonne was concerned that Cherie was selling herself short by taking this approach to her immediate future. By asking more questions about the sister, she discovered that before having her baby, she trained as a laboratory assistant and is planning to return to work in a few years. By considering her own long-term future through answering some 'what if ...' questions, Cherie could see that she might find it useful to invest in her future now to safeguard her prospects later. She went away with details about vocational courses in the sixth form, the address of the local technical college and an appointment with a local training scheme so she could look at all the options.

Three months later she is on a course at college which includes a work experience placement. She is planning the wedding for the day the course ends but is glad of the skills training she is getting.

Yvonne could be seen to be taking an interventionist approach here. She was not just an impartial mirror merely reflecting back her clients' wishes. She was aware of the fact that girls often neglect their career development through a lack of long-term planning, and so got her client to set her sights higher than she would otherwise have done. It is rarer for clients to aim too high. Most people do not push themselves far enough because of a lack of self-confidence.

If you ever do need to break the bad news to a client that he or she will not have the necessary ability in a certain area, perhaps because of anticipated low exam results, try to get clients to discover the point for themselves. There is well-produced careers information material available now for every job under the sun. These sheets or computerised programmes give full details about entry requirements and you can use them to get your clients discovering the facts of life for themselves, and then give them the scope to come back and discuss the implications with you later.

Chapter 4

Tools and Techniques

'I see careers guidance as helping people get to where they want to get to. They decide where that is and the best way to do it. The adviser helps generate the confidence to achieve it.'
Careers adviser, manager of an advice centre

As with any job, there are certain tools which can be used to make the work easier. These devices have been constructed to highlight aspects of ability, aptitude or interest to speed up the guidance process and improve the accuracy of advice given. Tools can take the shape of tests, guides or computer programmes for use by a client followed by analysis by an experienced and trained guidance worker.

Techniques are methods of helping clients understand their own backgrounds and the most suitable options available. They can take the form of written exercises, verbal triggers or suggested activities to focus a client on the most relevant factors to inform the decisions which will be made as a result. By suggesting a particular exercise, or offering testing facilities at an appropriate time in the guidance process, a careers advisor can help clients to navigate a faster and more direct path through the confusion of their total experience, skills and characteristics.

Psychological tests

Psychological tests are activities which can help to identify an individual's psychological attributes. These try to assess the general abilities of a person which may exist regardless of the qualifications or the skills acquired by that person. Tests are sold to practitioners and should be used by experienced and qualified advisers. They cannot solve the problem of making wise career decisions on their own, but can provide indicators of different abilities and suggestions for future direction. All tests need to be properly explained to clients in terms of how they work and what they can and cannot do.

Many clients believe that the point of seeking careers advice is to provide the right answer to the question of what to do next. Of course, there is never one correct next step, just an option which seems the best to the client concerned at that particular time. It is helpful to stress that any test will only come up with conclusions based on the known evidence, so it can speed up the analysis and make it logical, but cannot provide magic cures or solutions.

Sometimes clients will read far too much significance into test results and end up ignoring valid options because they were not indicated in the test results. A good adviser will strive to ensure that testing can have its place as one of a range of techniques available, but will guard against clients believing that it tells them what they must do. All tests have their proponents in the careers guidance field, whereas some advisers find that test use, despite being popular with clients, pigeon-holes an individual too quickly and prefer to conduct their work without them.

There are different types of tests. *Attainment* tests are designed to measure knowledge or skill levels and are not used to predict future performance in a job area, although they are sometimes used to match clients to types of vocational training. *Aptitude* tests assess the possible future capacity of a client to achieve in different abilities such as mechanical or technical areas. *Intelligence* tests look at general reasoning ability and problem-solving capacity. *Personality* tests are an attempt to describe the behaviour and character of the client and draw conclusions from the results to indicate how certain personality types will react to different environmental factors.

Someone may prove to have an ability in numerical reasoning, even if he or she has never studied mathematics, or shown any such prior propensity. Such tests are thought to demonstrate the relative strengths or capacities that a person might be able to demonstrate by scoring certain responses. Clients can find such tests useful for bringing out previously unknown strengths and may get to know themselves better as a result. Such tests should always be used in conjunction with an informed feedback session to explain and analyse the conclusions.

There are new and varied tests developing all the time, some with dubious scientific claims to accuracy. In an attempt to establish some quality standards the British Psychological Society provides a guide to the correct use of tests and the means by which their value can be assessed. They also emphasise that: 'The term Psychological Test should be restricted to assessment techniques yielding ratings of scores derived from procedures clearly described in the test manual and based on adequate standardisation data.' Test users should always be qualified to level A of the British Psychological Society Certificate of Competence in Occupational Testing.

Respected tests need to show that certain important factors have been addressed during the construction phase. These include the need for them to be reliable, have validity and relate to a known standard. Reliability is measured in terms of the consistency of a person reaching the same score at different times. Validity is a measure of how well a test indicates real ability through its scoring system, for example that a person scoring well in verbal reasoning will also perform well in a job using that ability. Tests need to relate all scores to a representative sample of the population in order to be standard.

The dangers of using badly designed or biased tests can be most easily understood when realising who uses tests. As well as careers advisers, who can have a major impact on a client's decisions if they give incorrect advice, tests are increasingly used by employers to decide who to recruit. Especially in periods of high unemployment, it can be useful for an employer or personnel department to have a convenient and relatively scientific way of eliminating a certain proportion of applicants for particular jobs. While this may seem sensible from the recruiters' point of view, it can be annoying and unfair to certain candidates to be ruled out on the basis of an analysis of the significance of their answers in a questionnaire.

One role of an adviser can be to help job candidates understand what tests are looking for when they form part of a recruitment process. Knowing that you have to sit a test for a job or training course can make people very nervous. Most careers offices or guidance centres will have examples of the sorts of questions to expect in order to help clients have an idea of what will happen on the appointed day. Some tests can discriminate on the grounds of race or sex by asking questions which are culturally biased and employers have been accused of inappropriate use of tests which discriminate against certain applicants.

Interest inventories

Less formal in design and less scientific in measurement, these are guides or indicators of vocational interest. These work by matching up client responses to a database of types of work. They can range from simple questionnaires to complex interrelational databases of job and activity analysis, but are trying to suggest suitable occupations for an individual as a response to significant questions about that client and his or her areas of career interest. A guide may try to narrow down choices by concentrating on certain limiting factors such as whether clients prefer working inside or outdoors, with others or alone, with their hands or with theoretical concepts etc. Some examples are Adult Directions, Microdoors and JIIGCAL. In a guidance setting these guides can be a useful tool if used for specific clients who express a desire to receive some suggestions about career ideas at the start of the decision-making process.

Often the result will be a list of possibly relevant career ideas which the client can then use to research more detail about what each job involves. The use of such interest inventories can be enjoyable, but clients may sometimes be disappointed at the outcome if the career ideas generated from their answers are too limited or seem far away from the sort of future they had imagined for themselves.

Paper exercises

Apart from talking to an adviser, it can sometimes be appropriate to take time out of a careers interview so that the client can do some work on paper to help identify significant factors. These written activities will often take the form of self-assessment work and can be undertaken as a sort of homework for the client to work on and return with at a subsequent interview.

The exercise on page 73 in Chapter 5 is a good example of this technique when a client is seeking help with job applications. Clients can be asked to put together a list of ten character strengths that they have, or skills that they have acquired or lessons that they have learned from their previous experience.

Another way of helping can be to ask your client to think through his or her life in terms of good and bad times. When did he enjoy his work most? Where was she happiest and most fulfilled? When did he struggle most? With whom did she most enjoy working? This information is only subjective but another dimension can be added by the client doing homework to ask friends, family and colleagues if they agree with the information he or she has come up with. A simple graph can be constructed to show satisfaction over time compared to different working environments, starting with school days and ending with the present situation.

One client may find that she has always been happiest when working in large teams, another that he spent the most rewarding times engaged on research work. One may long to relive the stimulating experience of studying at college, while another may see that manual work which can be left behind at the end of the day gave most satisfaction. When such a list is complete, it may be analysed to show why the experiences felt the way they did. Many clients will see for the first time how similar feelings are associated with similar experiences and how they are happiest in certain situations which can indicate a path to be followed for future satisfaction.

Some advisers try using pictures instead of words to help clients express their thoughts and feelings. You do not need an art degree to draw a pin figure in the middle of a large blank piece of paper and use coloured pens to outline what the client is aiming for. If the expectation of careers advice is to enable the client to see where he or she is going, sometimes seeing it drawn and listed on paper can be the most effective method.

A different kind of problem can exist when clients know themselves but cannot decide between two or more options. A written method of evaluating the choice can be a useful device here. For each choice, the client makes a list of the plus points and the minus points of going for that outcome. These can then be compared. Usually, one option has the greatest list of advantages and the smallest list of disadvantages – either in number or in their significance – which can make the choice an obvious one.

Mental exercises

The last device to help decision-making can be taken further if necessary by getting the clients to close their eyes and imagine they have moved through time five years after having plumped for one option. What are they doing? Get them to imagine their situation in the future. More importantly, looking back, how do they feel about the choice they made? They can then do the same mental exercise for another choice. Which one feels the better outcome? Which option do they regret not choosing most? What did they miss or lose out on in each case? The resulting feelings may be helpful for the client to evaluate the implications of the decision.

Job-hunting skills

We all need lots of encouragement when we are out of work, and a careers adviser can help to provide the structure and support necessary to a successful job search campaign. Many clients will benefit from ideas about the many different places to find out about jobs. Here are some examples:

- 70 per cent of jobs are never advertised – friends and family can often know of vacancies
- Employment agencies (not just for secretarial work)
- Jobcentres and careers offices
- Newspaper and local radio advertisements
- Cards in shop windows and community centre displays
- Articles and advertisements in professional or specialist journals and magazines.

When advisers are working with clients who are looking for employment, it can be useful to establish guidelines for a personal project to cover all the work that the client will need to do. A folder or file will be needed to hold all the paperwork that can be generated in such a search. If clients are in receipt of state benefits they will need to be able to prove at regular intervals that they are genuinely striving to find work. Such paper evidence can be essential in these cases, and it needs to be kept in order and in good condition.

Copies of job adverts, details of job descriptions and personnel specifications, copies of applications, CVs and letters sent to employers, together with any responses, should be neatly and carefully filed for future reference, with an index at the front if the file gets really cumbersome. A regular action list with dates of what the client will do and when, should be kept to ensure that speculative letters to employers asking about job vacancies are followed up at the appropriate time.

Chapter 5

CVs, Letters and Applications Forms

'You are only there to help the client. Your goals are not necessarily the same as theirs. Try not to make assumptions without checking them out with the client first.' **Career consultant working with adults**

One of the most important types of work that you can do for clients is give them the help that they need to apply for jobs. Particularly in recession, opportunities are all too few, and the numbers applying for vacancies are often in the hundreds for each job. As far as written applications and CVs are concerned there are three golden rules to impart to any client:

- Keep it simple
- Make it neat
- Give it impact.

CVs

First, a quick questionnaire to test your prior knowledge. Go through these ten questions using your own CV as an example. Find the statement that you think best answers each question. You may only select one answer for each.

CV Questionnaire

1. CV stands for —?

A) Complicated vocation
B) Career valuation
C) Curriculum vitae

2. A CV is for —?

A) Introducing yourself and your strengths in a formal manner
B) Pretending you are better than you really are
C) Sending to employers in order to get a job

3. Who should have a CV?

A) The unemployed
B) Everybody
C) School and college leavers

4. Which statement sums up what a CV is?

A) The story of your life – or those parts that employers want to know
B) A list of facts about your background
C) Your employment details

5. How long should a CV be?

A) A one page summary
B) As long as it takes to describe yourself adequately
C) Two pages preferably, but three if absolutely necessary

6. A CV should include — ?

A) Whatever you choose to select from your background
B) Every course, school and job that you have ever had
C) Anything; it will never be checked by employers

7. The appearance of your CV — ?

A) Is not as important as the content
B) Will not be hurt by a mistake or two
C) Is the most important thing about it

8. Your interests and hobbies should contain — ?

A) Nothing – they are not relevant to your working life and are none of the employer's business
B) Just two or three ordinary pastimes, for example 'watching television, socialising and reading'
C) Up to eight different things, preferably with one unusual interest

9. What about referees?

A) Two of the people who will give you the best references, including your present or last employer
B) At least three to show how popular you are, plus copies of any available certificates and testimonials
C) Not worth including, just put 'references available on request'

10. CV writing is — ?

A) Complicated and difficult, but a necessary evil
B) A time-consuming project which is ultimately satisfying
C) Easy – you can just copy somebody else's.

Questionnaire answers

1. CV Stands for — ?

C) Curriculum vitae

These words from Latin literally mean 'the course of your life'. Do not assume that everyone knows what they stand for. It is often helpful to clients if you can start off any work with them explaining its meaning and the different uses to which the document may be put.

2. A CV is for — ?

A) Introducing yourself and your strengths in a formal manner

Weaknesses are not needed here as the aim is to make the most of your experience and skills. Making the most of yourself is quite different from pretending you are better than you really are. The latter can cause problems at the interview stage when you are questioned in some detail about your work record. Even worse, you could get the job on the strength of some false claims and then be sacked when your employer finds out. There have been several cases of this happening when lies were discovered.

Although you can use your CV for sending to employers in order to get a job, it could also be useful for the following occasions:

- Applying for advertised vacancies when the employer specifies sending in a CV.
- Applying for vacancies in a speculative manner, or 'on spec'. This is when you write off to companies in the hope that they may have vacancies, now or in the future.
- For employment agencies when they are putting your name forward to the employers on their books.
- As a *aide-mémoire*, or as a memory-jogger, to save you remembering lists of relevant dates from your past when you are completing application forms.
- For general business purposes, when self-employed, doing consultancy work and so forth.
- As an introduction to organisations or banks when you need to explain your background for some purpose.

3. Who should have a CV?

B) Everybody

Everyone, including those who are unemployed and school and college leavers, should have an up-to-date and impressive CV of their own. You never know when the best job in the world may turn up and it is bound to be at the time in your life when you have no time to construct the document that you would like. Even if you have no plans to change jobs, you could use a CV for one of the purposes outlined in the answer to question 2. It is best to be prepared in advance, and a magnificent CV will do wonders for anybody's confidence in themselves.

4. Which statement sums up what a CV is?

A) The story of your life – or those parts that employers want to know

A list of facts about your background sounds rather dry doesn't it? This document needs to be very impressive at first reading. A list of events only will not inspire any reader. Although it should include employment details, it should also talk about educational background, skills and personality strengths to give a full picture of the author. After all, it is highly likely to be in a pile of 50 other CVs on an employer's desk and needs to convey a rounded picture of an unmissable candidate.

5. How long should a CV be?

C) Two pages preferably, but three if absolutely necessary

One of the most common mistakes when writing CVs is to make them too long. You will bore the reader if you write too much. There may be times when a brief, one page summary will suffice, but only when you are known to the reader already and not for most uses. The way to reduce the document is to edit ruthlessly. Use note form and only give space to those details that add to the total picture. Group together activities which do not need elaboration such as: 'I have also had holiday jobs in shops and restaurants'.

6. A CV should include — ?

A) Whatever you choose to select from your background

As explained in the answer to question 5, not every course, school and job that you have ever had need necessarily go in to a CV, although for someone with less work experience it will be useful not only to include every job but to build them up to stress the experience gained. Although it is true that the facts are seldom checked by employers, it may well come out by mistake when you have started the job, so do not invent material for any CV or encourage others to do so.

7. The appearance of your CV — ?

C) Is the most important thing about it

CVs that do not look good will not be read. Of course, the content is important but as that is only noticed after the appearance, you should spend time on the layout of a CV. There should be no spelling mistakes in the finished document. If, as an adviser, you can make facilities available for the use of clients to compile their own documents, you will be providing a popular service.

Nowadays it is important to get a CV typed on a word processor. This means that it can be updated easily later if it is saved on a disk and modern printing facilities can be used which have a far superior look to old typewriters.

8. Your interests and hobbies should contain — ?

C) Up to eight different things, preferably with one unusual interest

Although your interests outside work are your own business, they help to make some pieces of paper represent a living, breathing person who is worth interviewing. Watching television, socialising and reading, because they are what most of us do, are not going to grab the attention of the reader. Think back through your life about the activities that you used to spend time on, about the things you would like to do or the things that you never have time for. Try to include some interests which use your brain, some which are more practical and something out of the ordinary.

9. What about referees?

A) Two of the people who will give you the best references, including your present or last employer

Copies of any available certificates and testimonials will only clutter up a CV. Keep those back until an interested employer asks to see them. The exception is if the only references available are from another country. It is a rare employer who will bother writing abroad to obtain these, except for the most senior jobs, so you will need to get open testimonials headed up: 'To whom it may concern' in this case. Just putting 'references available on request' only creates a hurdle between you and an employer and your CV risks being rejected. Give full details including telephone numbers of your two referees but check first that they are agreeable to you putting their names forward.

10. CV writing is — ?

B) A time-consuming project which is ultimately satisfying

It is indeed complicated and difficult, particularly when starting to produce a document either for yourself or a client but if it secures the job of your choice it can earn you thousands of pounds. Treat CV compilation as a major, fulfilling project, useful in the end even though lengthy and challenging in the doing. There is no short cut to a good document which will make an employer sit up and want to meet you. If you copy somebody else's document, be aware that you will not be taking the opportunity to do yourself justice and may sacrifice the chance of the job you want.

How to work with clients

These questionnaire answers have, in the main, related to your own CV, but I hope it is clear that the answers will be the same ones that you can give to your clients when they want to know how to approach the task of starting their job search by creating the best CV they can, with your help.

The CV is a flexible and self-defined tool which can increase the confidence and employment prospects of your client. Because the client ultimately chooses what to put in the CV and what to leave out, it is a personal document. Unlike an application form where we all have to obey the employer's instructions to complete the boxes on the form, with a CV the writer decides what to put down. Because of this, it can seem hard work for clients and this is one area of your work where you can give straight advice about a good way to lay out the document. My earlier book, *Preparing Your Own CV*, gives ten examples of different CVs but the way I recommend laying the document out is shown on pages 74–75.

As careers adviser, you should not be writing your clients' CVs for them or taking them through each stage as they complete the document. By all means briefly explain what type of information you think should be included and then let them do the work for themselves. Your role is to help edit, encourage trumpet-blowing and to discuss layout and presentation. I recommend taking clients through compiling a CV in two stages – first content and then presentation.

A blank form (see pages 76–77) can be used by your clients to start them off. At this first draft stage, encourage them to include anything and everything that they have done, without worrying too much about layout and spelling. The information can be cut down and tidied up later.

Be sensitive to the particular details of your client's history. People without qualifications need to stress the subjects that they studied at school or college, to get credit for what they have achieved. Encourage CV writers to include anything which will make them stand out from the crowd. Educational projects completed, voluntary work done, unusual interests or attainments in the workplace will all be important here. The employment section should be written in reverse chronological order, most recent job first. The main duties should consist of action verbs in list form, to outline quickly the main features of the job.

The other skills section is often overlooked, but can include computer literacy, driving licence, first aid, languages; anything which the client knows about but which would not necessarily show up anywhere else in the document.

The additional information section is the way to make a CV different from others in the pile on the employer's desk. It is also a chance to explain gaps in the document. If your client has been out of the employment market for some reason it can be covered here, or if he or she has been travelling around the world, this is the chance to describe what the experience has taught them. First get your clients to list ten good things about themselves, particularly those characteristics which relate to the world of work. How would the person who loves them most in the world describe them?

Most clients will find this excruciatingly difficult. The most confident individual will end up blushing and frowning while struggling to compile ten little words on the list. Try it for yourself.

1. ________________________
2. ________________________
3. ________________________
4. ________________________
5. ________________________
6. ________________________
7. ________________________
8. ________________________
9. ________________________
10. ________________________

Once written, this list will be the basis for this section of the CV, for application form answers and for interview questions. Every client should be motivated to reach ten items.

CURRICULUM VITAE

NAME:	**Marilyn BROWNE**	
ADDRESS:	806 Tiverton Place London N5 2HX	
TELEPHONE:	000–000 0000	
DATE OF BIRTH:	20 May 1960	
MARITAL STATUS:	Divorced	
NATIONALITY:	British	
HEALTH:	Excellent	

EDUCATION:

1973– 1978	Ragdale School Birmingham B14 1LJ	**O levels:** English A, Biology B, Maths B, History C, Chemistry B
1978– 1980	Charing Court Hospital London W5 2JN	**Pupil Nurse for State Enrolled Nurse**
1991	Queen's Hospital London SE3 2HJ	**Conversion Course to Registered Nurse**

EMPLOYMENT:

Nov 1987– Jan 1993	Queen's Hospital London SE3 2HJ	**State Enrolled Nurse and Registered Nurse:** Working in theatre with the Sister, making sure theatre list is correctly written, that theatre is ready for use, instruments are correct for different operations, teaching student nurses, completing appropriate paperwork, liaising between hospital departments

June 1984– Aug 1987	Waterside Hospital London W1 3PP	**State Enrolled Nurse:** Looking after medical and surgical patients, doing ward rounds with doctors, updating patients' notes, transferring patients to theatre, dealing with enquiries, dispensing drugs.
Nov 1980– May 1984	Charing Court Hospital London W5 2JN	**State Enrolled Nurse:** Working in out-patients department, making sure patients' notes were completed, getting doctors' trays ready for examination, answering phone calls, dealing with patients and medical sales representatives.

INTERESTS:
Horse-riding, badminton, walking my dog, reading nursing journals.

ADDITIONAL INFORMATION:
My working life to date has been mainly caring for people. This has made me patient and tolerant when dealing with the public. In hospital, patients and their relatives are often scared and distressed, even angry, and they need calm but firm handling.
As a result of my State Enrolled Nurse training, I am familiar with the study of biology, chemistry and drugs, and have had 13 years' experience as a qualified nurse working in a variety of different medical establishments.
I wish to use my professional skills in combination with my main interest, which is caring for animals. I feel my nursing skills together with my trustworthy and dedicated character, would make me ideally suited to a career as an animal nurse.

REFERENCES

Mr Simon Howarth (Theatre Manager) Queen's Hospital London SE3 2HJ Tel: 000 000 0000	Mrs J Michaels 21 Green Vale London SE16 2KY Tel: 000 000 0000

Blank CV

CURRICULUM VITAE

NAME:

ADDRESS:

TELEPHONE NUMBER:

DATE OF BIRTH:

NATIONALITY:

MARITAL STATUS:

EDUCATION:

(Dates) (Name and location) (Qualifications or subjects studied)

EMPLOYMENT:

(Dates) (Name and location) (Position held and main duties)

OTHER SKILLS:

INTERESTS:

ADDITIONAL INFORMATION:

REFERENCES:

From these ten, perhaps six could be extracted to be the core of this section. Let us assume your six most appropriate words were:

1. creative
2. practical
3. adaptable
4. quick to learn
5. patient
6. hardworking

If you were my client I would then get you to form these into a couple of short paragraphs for your section, with illustrations if possible. If you were a recent school leaver you might end up with something like this:

I am a practical and creative person. I make all my own clothes and helped to build a kit car last year which took a lot of patience. I am adaptable to changing circumstances and when I had to move schools recently, I enjoyed making new friends and soon fitted in.

One of my favourite subjects is technical drawing. I help out in my uncle's garage at weekends and work hard to look after the shop there for him. I get on well with all his customers and would like to gain some experience in a larger retail store.

Presentation

The way the document is presented is the most important aspect of it, even more so than what it says. Without looking good it will not be read, particularly not in our present competitive job market. It needs to look immaculate. This means that hand-written CVs are out. You should be aiming to get all clients to use word processors or, at the very least, a typewriter. Apart from anything else, a document on computer can be painlessly amended and updated.

Use the order of layout in my example above. It seems to strike a chord with most employers. Pay particular attention to the use of capital letters and bold type. The computer-mad among your client group will try to garnish their documents with borders, multiple font styles and frills. Hold them back by reminding them that for any written document, as long as it is neat, *simple is best*.

Do not let the document stray over two sides of A4 of

white or cream paper unless the client has had many different jobs or is older. *Nobody* should take more than three pages. If in doubt about whether to include a piece of information, be ruthless and edit it out. Try to impress on your clients that spelling mistakes are unacceptable. They should always check and re-check completed forms for errors and mistyped words. This will take time but having an impressive and up-to-date CV will pay dividends one day, and not just in terms of the increased self-confidence that its compilation brings.

Covering letters

Lastly, once the perfect CV exists, make sure your client uses it frequently and properly – never without a covering letter. Such a letter really introduces and sells the CV itself and therefore it needs to be bold, confident and clear. Ideally, it should not go over two sides in length and should include the following:

- Why you are sending the CV
- Significant things about your background and skills
- The sort of person you are
- What you can offer the organisation (not what you want from them)
- What you would like to happen next
- How you can be contacted.

Some examples are given on the following pages.

I Speculative approach

Maria MacDonald
Basement Flat
2 Arbour Fields
Richmond
N Yorkshire

15 April 1994

Mr David Belton
Director
Salcott Equipment
33 Pinks Lane
Richmond
N Yorkshire

Dear Mr Belton

I am writing to enquire if you have any vacancies in your company. I enclose my CV for your information. As you can see, I have spent ten years working with a variety of different machinery and equipment and am used to industrial work.

I am a steady and serious person who works hard and fits easily into a new team. I am clean and careful in my work and can lend a hand in the office when needed. I am quick to pick up new instructions and flexible about the hours that I work. It was normal for me to do shift-work in my last job. I am known for taking a pride in my work and want to work for a company with a reputation for producing quality goods – hence my application to Salcott's.

I have excellent references and would be delighted to discuss any possible vacancy with you at your convenience. In case you do not have any suitable openings at the moment, I would be grateful if you would keep my CV on file for any future possibilities.

Thank you for your attention to this matter. I look forward to hearing from you.

Yours sincerely

Maria MacDonald

Enc:

2 College leaver

Adrian Miller
97 Potter's Close
Sedgefield
Teesside
RT3 3PP

25 October 1994

Ms Louise Powell
Powell's Energy Company
200 Seymour Industrial Estate
Hartfield Road
Middlesbrough GT99 1LZ

Dear Ms Powell

Please find enclosed my CV in application for the post advertised in the *Guardian* on 20 October.

The nature of my degree course has prepared me for this position. The course involved a great deal of independent research, relying on a substantial amount of translating into French and Spanish. I also studied economic history and for one course (History of Latin America since Independence) an understanding of the petro-chemical industry was essential. I found this subject very stimulating.

I am a fast and accurate writer, with a keen eye for detail and I should be very grateful for the opportunity to progress to market reporting.

I have not only the ability to take on the responsibility of this position immediately, but I believe that I also have the enthusiasm and determination to ensure that I make a success of it.

Thank you for taking the time to consider this application and I look forward to hearing from you in the near future.

Yours sincerely

Adrian Miller

Enc:

3 Woman returner

Sherena Williams
Hazelwood Cottage
Sandy Hill
Sway
Hampshire

13 December 1994

The Personnel Manager
Hall's Ltd
100 London Road
Brockenhurst
Hampshire

Dear Sir/Madam

Re: Accounts Manager Vacancy

I am writing in reply to your advertisement in this week's *Hampshire Times*. I enclose my CV for your information. As you can see, I trained in accounting at Bishop's Technical College gaining a BTEC pass in 1984. For the next four years I ran the accounts department of Nicholson's Bakery in Lymington. I covered the whole variety of work in this busy office, from handling petty cash and making wage payments to credit control.

I left this post in 1988 to bring up my two young children. Being a full-time parent has enabled me to acquire new skills, such as scheduling and keeping to deadlines, organising, communicating on different levels, delegating work and using my creative imagination to solve problems.

I am patient and flexible, stay calm in difficult situations, and am confident when working with figures and running an office. I am hard-working and thorough and am looking forward to resuming my career with a pace-making organisation like Hall's.

I would be happy to discuss this application in more detail and look forward to hearing from you.

Yours faithfully

Sherena Williams

Enc:

4 School/College leaver

Fola Okintola
111 Poulton Terrace
Sidcup
Kent

1 September 1994

The Personnel Director
Haddleston Council
Haddleston
Kent

Dear Sir/Madam

Re: Vacancies for Junior Trainees

I would like to apply for the vacancy for junior trainee which I saw in my local careers office.

I left Cole Comprehensive School this year after taking my GCSE exams. I passed in English, Mathematics and General Science and won a prize for a project on 'Science and Ecology' earlier in my final year. I enclose a copy of my CV and my Record of Achievement which shows my progress throughout the last two years.

I am good at bringing the best out of other people and spent my sports lessons at school being a key player in the volleyball team. I have worked each summer for the last three years as an assistant in the local sports centre helping to organise the summer sports programme which the Council runs each year for school children. I am interested in working for the Council because I believe that local services are important. I take a pride in living in this area and know that your recent Quality Initiative has made people realise how much they depend on good street lighting and cleaning, housing and leisure facilities.

I would like to become a part of the team of people who organise such services and look forward to discussing how I can contribute to the work of the Council in due course.

Thank you for your time. I look forward to hearing from you.

Yours faithfully

Fola Okintola

Enc:

5 Mature candidate

Louis Coombe
80 Bryan Ridge
Westminster Parade
London SW15

15 February 1994

Mrs Alberga
Personnel Manager
Kogan and Company
Norman Street
London W1

Dear Mrs Alberga

Re: Adviser, Training Unit

Please find enclosed my CV. I have had many years' successful experience as a personnel manager in the clothing industry. Working with teams of different people meant that I quickly became adaptable and flexible.

I am at present updating my computer skills at a local resource centre and I have been helping the tutors there, on a voluntary basis, with the new trainees. I introduce them to the centre and act as a mentor during their training programme.

I devote time to making sure that everyone works well together and can recognise problems before they become insurmountable. I am approachable and tolerant but maintain high standards and the ability to communicate quickly and clearly with others. I am known for my ability to make learning fun and can always motivate people to give more of themselves. My mature outlook allows me to be a soothing influence at difficult times and I have a wide experience of work to draw on when needed.

I would enjoy contributing to the training provided by your company as I know of your excellent reputation in this field. I have a relative who works in your Northern Region who tells me that your staff development programme is very good.

I would be delighted to discuss any detail of my application at your convenience. Thank you for your attention to this matter. I look forward to hearing from you.

Yours sincerely

Louis Coombe

Enc:

Application forms

Advising about application forms calls on many of the lessons learnt about compiling CVs. The most important point is to drum into every client's head that every application that ever gained an applicant a job was:

NEATLY WRITTEN with NO SPELLING MISTAKES.

Application forms take a long time to complete properly and should always be written out in draft before the neat top copy is attempted. For each page of the form, your client should allow a day's preparation and work. Typing forms should be left to the experts but capital letters can improve the appearance of most handwriting.

What the employer is looking for

Employers have a difficult time during the selection process trying to decide who to interview from the evidence on pieces of paper alone. That is why so many make use of application forms. That way they can specify the questions to be answered and compare like with like once the forms are returned. It makes it harder for the candidates as they have far less discretion about what to say than with a CV that they have designed for themselves.

Because the employer has designed the form, it is important to try and see the job from his or her point of view in order to stand a chance of being picked to attend an interview. We have already said that all employers are interested in three things:

- Skills
- Experience
- Personality

and your forms need to demonstrate:

- What you can offer the organisation.

Given a range of candidates all of whom can demonstrate

relevant skills and appropriate experience, the interviews will be scheduled for those candidates whose forms show that they have attractive and suitable personalities. This means that your client must analyse what the job involves.

Using the advertisement, the job description and personnel specification, if they exist, and any other material that can be gathered about the organisation and that particular job the candidate needs to draw up a picture of the person the employer is looking for. By picking out the verbs in the material it can be seen what the job mainly consists of and therefore what sort of person would be able to carry it out. A person specification is a real gift – a bit like knowing the questions in advance of an exam, as it tells you exactly the sort of person required. Your client needs to prove he or she has all the attributes listed.

How to work with clients

The most important thing is to give clients sufficient support and encouragement to blow their own trumpets loudly. A nice but unexciting impression will not get an invitation to an interview. A successful application implies that all events have been leading the applicant to apply for this job at this time and that the employer would be mad to miss meeting the person concerned. This requires the literary equivalent of shouting loudly about every strength and achievement. Use the same list of ten things from page 73 to get clients armed with positive comments about themselves which can then be used for the difficult question, 'please explain why you think you would be suitable for this position' or however it is worded.

Chapter 6

The Interview

'Don't worry about not knowing everything about your client. Create the right atmosphere between you and ask open questions to get them talking.' **Tutor with a training provider**

Giving clients guidance about interview techniques is all about conveying a measure of self-confidence. However, merely getting the answers right is not enough and clients have to be made aware of the significance of image and body language, facial expression and handling nerves.

How to help the client

If your client has made several job applications and is getting job interviews but then having no success at being offered a position, it is likely that his or her interview technique needs attention. There are two ways of helping your clients. The first involves getting them to see the whole question of interviews from the employer's point of view. Many clients will have attended very few interviews, so the more information that you can give them the better.

What employers are looking for

Employers want to know what an applicant has to offer the organisation. In a recession particularly, when applicants for jobs are plentiful, successful candidates have to explain themselves in terms of what they will contribute to the work of the company concerned. Everyone who applies will want to get the job and earn the wage or salary, but why should the employer choose one person over another? The impression that needs to be created is one of everything in the candidate's life leading him or her to this point where he or she is on offer to this employer. This may sound difficult to convey, but the right mixture of preparation, enthusiasm and confidence can make a candidate seem too good to forgo.

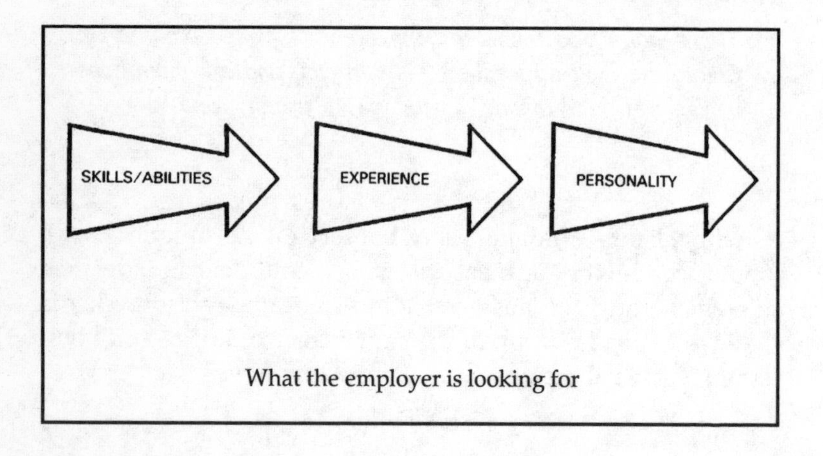

What the employer is looking for

Handling nerves

The second idea for making your clients feel more confident about their performance in an interview situation is to convey the fact that most interviewers are themselves very nervous and can often be bad at conducting interviews.

For clients, planning and preparation can eliminate some of the nerve strain, and clients should be encouraged to practise their interview answers as much as possible with you, friends or by themselves in front of a mirror. As a follow-on exercise to that described on page 75, get your clients to read out loud their list of ten character strengths. Everyone finds this awkward and difficult (even if they claim not to). That very difficulty is why the effort will be so worthwhile. If someone can get used to describing themselves in terms of good points and benefits, they will be prepared to answer the interview question 'Why should we employ you?' with more confidence and aplomb.

You can encourage clients to explore ways of handling their nerves. Simple breathing exercises, stretching the mouth and face before an interview and a good posture can all help the body to cope with stressful situations.

Image, body language and facial expression

Careers advisers should spend as much time advising clients about their image as about the content of their interview answers. Evidence shows that most job interviews are decided by the impression that the employer gets of each candidate in the first 30 seconds. Clients who can make their appearance clean, tidy, well coordinated and with some sign of style are at a distinct advantage. Many books have been written on the significance of image and it is worth careers advisers looking into this fascinating subject.

Use the following guidelines as advice to job interview candidates and they will not go wrong.

General

- Wear good quality clothes that fit. If in doubt about size, go one larger
- Dark colours (navy blue and dark grey) carry more authority than lighter colours, but avoid black unless you have dark colouring
- Carry a brief case or bag but not both
- Hair should be clean and well cut
- Fingernails should be short and clean
- Shoes should be clean.

Men

- Wear plain, long-sleeved shirts (white or pastel shades) with ordinary collars (not buttoned down)

- The brightest white shirts only suit those with the darkest colouring; keep to a softer ivory or just off-white
- The point of your tie should touch the waistband of your trousers
- Wear knee-length dark socks and black, lace-up shoes
- Do not wear a sweater under your jacket
- Use after-shave and cologne sparingly in the day
- Facial hair, if you must have it, should be trim
- Have your tie straight
- Wear a bald patch with pride
- No jewellery except a sensible watch.

Women

- Wear a jacket or a suit
- Keep patterns to a minimum
- No very high heels
- Tie long hair back neatly to look older or less frivolous
- Flesh-coloured tights or the same colour as skirt and shoes
- Minimum jewellery that does not distract from you
- Skirt and jacket in dark, neutral colours, top in a light colour
- Make-up can help for creating a more authoritative look
- Sparing use of perfume during the day.

Most people need help with understanding what body language is and how powerful it can be as a means of communicating our feelings. You will need to demonstrate to your clients the different effects of crossed arms, scowling, upright posture and smiling. The first two will send out negative statements at interview and the last two should always be in evidence. If you do not tell interview candidates about their irritating mannerisms, nobody else will either and their hair twisting or finger tapping might lose them that job.

The mock interview

Wherever possible, run through the interview with your

client. Many advisers worry about offering this service because they feel unsure about what questions to ask. They swot up on the technical details of the job concerned and completely miss the point of the exercise. What you are trying to do here is make your client feel more confident about the whole process. Their demeanour and attitude are far more important than the words that they say. Get your clients to concentrate on body language and give them feedback afterwards on how they came over.

It is helpful if your client has a particular job in mind before you practise in this way, as the lessons will be more significant, but even if he or she only has an idea of the sort of job that could be applied for, a chance to experiment with different answers should be very valuable. Most employers decide on their attitude to your client in the first 30 seconds of them entering the room. The majority of that impression will be gained from the way the client looks and his or her body language.

These five points should be your objectives:

1. Ask general questions to get your clients to concentrate on selling themselves.
2. Encourage your clients to structure answers so that they offer three main points where possible.
3. Make sure they keep waffle down to the minimum, but nonetheless speak clearly and give full answers.
4. Show them that they can anticipate questions before any interview and can plan their answers accordingly.
5. Get them to illustrate their *skills*, *experience* and *personality* through what they say.

With you acting as the interviewer, play it as straight as possible, asking the questions politely but firmly, as though you have not met your interviewee before. After each question or at the end of the whole event, you can revert to being yourself to ask the 'candidate' how he or she thought the answer went, and then you can add your constructive comments. At all times build up your client and encourage him or her to answer fully. Praise the good answers and only offer positive suggestions about improving answers even more when you convey your impression. If clients feel that they have done well with you, then the experience of the real thing will not seem so daunting.

Examples of interview questions and answers*

Here is a selection of typical questions that may be asked in an interview. Following each question are some suggestions about the type of information that the interviewer would be interested in as part of the answer. Interviewees will rarely be asked *all* these questions, but as full a range as possible has been included. If your clients can answer all these questions confidently they are truly ready for their interview!

A full answer for each question has been suggested. These questions are only being asked to prompt the interviewees to talk about themselves. The more information they can give, the more helpful it will be, as long as the answers are concise, clear and relevant. Details are not as important as stressing what skills or experience they have gained.

The following questions and commentaries on them are directed at your client. You may wish to run through the questions as part of preparation for a feedback from a mock interview.

Education and training

1. Why did you decide to go to college?
This requires a full answer, and you need to go back to when you left school in order to be able to answer it. What were your long-term ambitions at the time? Were there certain subjects you particularly enjoyed at school and wished to continue to study? How and why did you choose your particular course and your specialist subjects?

* The text is derived from *Successful Interview Skills* by Rebecca Corfield (Kogan Page, 1992).

2. Can you tell me about your college course?

Many people forget to explain exactly where they went to college and precisely which course they took. Even if the employer already has this information on your CV or application form, he or she may not have it to hand, or even remember having seen it before. What sort of teaching methods were employed? Were there compulsory core subjects and specialist options? How did you decide which to study?

3. Did you enjoy any particular part of your studies more than the rest?

The employer is trying to find out what sort of person you are to get clues about the sort of work that would suit you best. Was there some particular option or course that you enjoyed more than others? Did it involve working alone or with other people?

Talking at length about how much you enjoyed researching alone in the chemistry laboratory at college will indicate your preferred style of working. The interviewer will probably assume that you are not the team player that he or she is looking for.

4. Can you tell me about a project that you worked on at school or college?

Working life is full of dealing with projects of one kind or another, from getting a letter typed, to managing a building contract, to supervising a team of accounts clerks. This question is being asked because the answer will give an indication of the way you would deal with this kind of work. You will need to explain how the project was conceived, what the task was, who else was involved in the work, how you worked together, how you handled any difficulties and what you think you gained from the exercise.

Employment history

5. Have you had any work experience?

This question is often asked of younger people who have just left full-time education. No employer wants to hear that you are completely inexperienced, even if you only left college a week ago. You will need to come up with some kind of answer in order to reassure the interviewer that you are used to the routine of work, that you can hold a position and that someone else has wanted to employ you in the past. Perhaps you have done a paper round; worked on voluntary projects while at school; had holiday or vacation jobs or participated in a work experience programme at school.

If you have never done any type of work at all, now is the time to start. You could offer your services to a community organisation on a voluntary basis or 'work shadow' some friend or relative who does what you are interested in. If you are studying it may be possible to get a Saturday or evening job. Apart from providing you with a positive response to this question, the work experience may gain you a character reference from the organisation concerned.

6. Can you tell me about your last job?

Again, it is not the precise details of what you were doing in the job that are wanted, but an account of the main skills involved and what you contributed to the organisation. Give concrete examples where possible to illustrate your points and stress how you have progressed in the course of the job.

7. Why did you leave your last position?

This is not the time to decry either your last job, the people you worked with or the employer concerned. A candidate who appears to have difficulty in getting on with people will definitely not be offered the position. Nobody wants to risk employing a trouble-maker. You will need to provide positive reasons for moving on from your last job, involving either different work or preferably taking up a new opportunity – to study, do voluntary work, or whatever you say you have been doing since you stopped work. If there were major problems in your last (or present) job that you wish to mention, you should only talk about possible improvements which could be made in order to sound positive.

If you are currently employed, make sure that you do not

sound desperate to escape from your job. You must provide positive illustrations of the way you could contribute to the position for which you have applied.

8. What have you been doing since you left your last job?

This is a good question which you can easily use to your advantage. If you are not working, and even if you have been unemployed for some time, you must come up with something positive that you have been doing with your time since you last worked. It is not enough to say that you have been looking for another job – that will be assumed.

The best answer will be either that you have been doing some sort of course to improve your skills or that you have been doing some voluntary work. If you know someone who runs a business, it may be possible to say that you have been doing some freelance contract work, helping out with this company.

Whatever you say will need to be backed up with details of your activities, if the employer wishes to know more. If you are not doing anything with your time – you must start something immediately. Apart from being an absolute necessity for your CV and job applications, it is the perfect antidote to the depression that can come with unemployment.

9. What has been your greatest achievement in your working history?

Some hard thinking before the interview is needed in order to answer this question. The example that you choose should convey some of the principal qualities needed in the job applied for and should be explained clearly and concisely.

10. Can you tell me about a problem that you have had to deal with?

The point of this question, as far as the employer is concerned, is to see how you would tackle obstacles at work. An ideal answer would involve you in thinking through a difficulty and solving it with the help of other people. If you can indicate some general lessons that you learnt from the experience, so much the better.

11. What would you do if you had a problem that you could not deal with? Perhaps you are faced with a difficult customer.

Everybody has to ask for help at times during their working lives. Your answer should show that you would not give up as soon as you were faced with a problem. The employer wants to see that you would be responsible and calm in your dealings with customers. Explain that you would try to find out the exact nature of the problem troubling the customer, while calming him or her down, if necessary.

Tell the interviewer that you are aware that you would need all the details in order to pass them on to whoever could sort out the problem. Apologising to the customer for the delay, you would tell him or her exactly when the problem would be attended to. You would then pass on the query to your supervisor or the person responsible.

12. Which of all your jobs have you found the most interesting, and why?

This question may be asked if you have had a varied employment history. A wise answer would include work similar to the job on offer to show that you will be happy and involved in your work. Try to justify your choice by giving examples of your main achievements in the time spent there, or explaining the particularly interesting aspects.

13. What are the most satisfying and the most frustrating aspects of your present/last job?

You may be asked this question to find out what you like best and least about your most recent position. Think carefully before you phrase your answer. The most satisfying aspects of the job should be those most closely linked to the position that you are now applying for. A long list of frustrations can make you sound like a moaner. If there was some particularly difficult aspect of the job, try to say how you helped to improve it.

Interests

14. What hobbies or interests do you have?

Why should employers be interested in the answer to this question? Is it pure nosiness? Everything you say about yourself contributes to the general impression gained about you. If I tell you that my hobbies are knitting, cookery, needlework, decorating cakes and bird-watching, you have an idea of the sort of person I am. If, however, I tell you that my hobbies include karate, African music, organising a community group, gardening and swimming, the picture is quite different.

You need to think hard about which hobbies and interests to mention. They can illustrate that you have a well-rounded personality and lead a full and satisfying life. Examples of times when you were in a leading or organising role will create a good impression.

There are some interests that we all have in common and these are not worth listing. We all read, watch television and socialise with other people, and these activities should not be part of your answer unless you have something specific to say about them. Be warned that if you mention them, you are likely to be asked either 'What was the last book you read?' or 'Can you tell me about a television programme that interested you lately?' Details of the latest episode of your favourite soap opera will not suffice!

Do not be too specific about any political or religious interests unless they are of direct relevance to the job in question. It is better just to say, as in the example above, that you are actively involved in the local community. The interviewer may hold different views from your own.

You do not have to spend time on all the hobbies that you mention, but be sure that you know enough to talk about the subject in some depth. Employers often pick on hobbies as an easy area of questioning and will be interested in discussing more unusual choices.

You should have some knowledge of every hobby that you mention, even if you need to say: 'Well, I am very interested in wind-surfing. At the moment I am finding out about it, but I intend to spend some time next summer having a go,' or 'I used to play a lot of basketball at school. I'm a bit rusty now, but I watch it when I can and am joining an evening class shortly to brush up my skills.'

The three points to be aware of when answering this question are:

- Include a variety of interests – some using your mind and some sporting or physical activities to show that you are a lively, healthy and active person.
- Ensure that you have at least one pastime which is different from other people's.
- Be prepared to discuss any of the topics you mention in some detail.

General

15. What are your strengths?

A favourite question. If you were ever given a chance to shine – this is it. Although at first sight this seems daunting, it is easy to prepare an impressive answer if you consider it before the interview.

Refer back to your list of good qualities on page 73. This list is very useful as the basis for answering any question about your strengths. By selecting five or six points from your list, you can put together a clear and powerful answer. Because you have prepared in advance, you will sound confident about your own abilities and proud of your character.

Examples could be: 'Flexible; good at keeping to deadlines; calm; can work under pressure ...' and so forth.

16. What are your weaknesses?

Whatever does the employer mean by asking this question? Nobody will want to employ someone who can reel off a long list of serious faults. The best way to answer is not to admit to any weaknesses at all. If you do mention weaknesses, make sure that they are those which sound more like strengths. For instance: 'I sometimes take my work too seriously and will stay late at the office to get something finished', or 'I tend to be very flexible as a work colleague, and I will do the jobs that no one else wants to do'. No employer will mind you having weaknesses like these!

17. What are you most proud of?

This should normally relate to some work experience, and it is helpful if it can demonstrate the necessary qualities for the job on offer. Any project or team work where you played a significant role could be mentioned. Any instance where your contribution made a real difference, where you tried an innovative approach or learnt something new would be well worth mentioning.

18 Which current affairs problem have you been aware of lately?

This is a favourite question for civil service jobs and is designed to check two things. The first is that your understanding of the world is wide and up to date, and the second is to see what sort of political attitudes you have. It therefore makes sense to read a quality daily newspaper thoroughly for at least a week before any interview. This is particularly relevant when you have applied for a job where you would be representing the views of the employing organisation.

Employers rarely want candidates to express strong political views in interviews. This is particularly true of the civil service and local authorities. Ideally, you should illustrate that you know about a current issue in some depth, you are aware of the different sides to the argument, you can understand the feelings on both sides and you realise what a difficult political problem it is.

Politics should be left to politicians and our private lives, not brought into the workplace. If you are asked for your opinion on a political issue, refrain from coming down heavily on either side. Government or local authority employers want to be sure that you are aware of the need to put into practice the wishes of the political masters of the day – and they can be right or left wing.

19. What do you see yourself doing in five years' time?

This is a similar question to one about your career ambitions. Think – why is the employer asking this? Does he or she want to know that you plan to train as an accountant or an actor in your spare time, and leave this job as soon as possible? No. He or she wants a member of staff who is serious about the vacancy and interested in staying put for a considerable time. Your answer could indicate that you hope to be in the company, but perhaps with greater responsibilities.

20. Why should we employ you rather than another candidate?

This is another good question as it enables you to use your list of ten strengths again. (See question 15 above.) Employers are interested in hearing about your skills, experience and personality.

In your answer you could mention any of your particular skills which relate to the job, your relevant experience, and add those aspects of your personality which best suit you for the position. A question like this is a gift to an interviewee. Do not be worried about boasting. This is the time to 'sell yourself' strongly to the interviewer. You are being asked to summarise your application – and the answer to this question is the crux of the whole interview.

21. What other careers are you interested in?

If you are applying for a computer operator's job in order to pay the rent and secretly want to be a police officer or a ballet dancer, keep that to yourself. Again, think – why is the employer interested in this question? He or she will be most impressed by the candidate who seems serious about the job on offer and about making a career in this line of work. Imply that your career ambitions are in this exact field. You could add that in the future you would be interested in working your way up to a position with more responsibility, or perhaps specialising in a particular area of the work.

22. Which other organisations have you applied to?

This question is similar to the one above. The employer does not want a candidate whom every other company has rejected. You want to convey the impression that you feel this particular vacancy is exactly the right one for you, and you have been saving yourself for it. I recommend that you say you are being choosy about the companies you approach. In other words, imply that you have not found such an interesting vacancy as this before.

23. What does equal opportunities mean to you?

This is the most difficult question to answer. But, fortunately, most interviewers are not too sure what the correct answer is. As long as you demonstrate that you understand the importance of everyone getting the same chances in employment and access to services, the employer will be impressed.

Many people answer: 'Treating everyone in the same way.' I think this answer is a little too simple. Some people with special needs may need extra help. You may have some personal awareness of this subject and feel like expressing it in the interview. For instance: 'As a woman, I know how it feels not to be taken seriously sometimes, so I always try to make sure that I treat everyone with respect,' or 'When I first arrived in this country I felt like an outsider and I am keen to help those who may need more support to make full use of the services offered by this organisation.'

24. How would you put equal opportunities into practice?

This is often asked together with the previous question. The trick is to think about the best answer in the light of the organisation applied to. Why has the employer decided to ask you this? It is likely that the current vacancy is with a large organisation, public company or local authority which is looking for staff who will be aware of two things: first, that services need to be made available to the whole population and, second, that colleagues may need support and understanding too. Explain how you would aim to fulfil these requirements in that job.

The vacancy

25. Tell me what you know about this organisation.

There is no excuse for not having a response to this question. Whatever the particular job that you are applying for, the interviewer will expect you to have some knowledge of the organisation, and the more the better. Whether you have seen an advertisement, been sent a job description or person specification, or read literature about the company, you should have some information to offer. The more you know, the more suitable you will seem.

26. Why do you want to work for this company?

Answering this question depends on the type of work offered and how much you know about the company concerned. You need to stress the particular type of organisation in relation to your own skills, strengths and personality.

27. If you were offered this job, how do you think you would spend your first two weeks with the company?

This is a more general question designed to check that you have a realistic and sensible approach to work. In most jobs, unless you have worked for the organisation before, you need to spend your first few days getting used to the new environment. This means finding your way around, meeting your new colleagues, and familiarising yourself with the rules and working practices. You would also probably spend some time with your new manager learning how the work is done and about current priorities.

28. What do you think are the most important issues facing this organisation at the moment?

This question may well be posed when certain political or financial issues affect an organisation. Examples of such organisations could be charities, pressure groups or local authorities. Your answer would depend on the exact nature of the employer, but could include: generating income; allocating scarce resources; setting objectives; implementing cutbacks; quality control; managing grant-funding or some particular campaign that the organisation is involved with.

29. What do you think you can contribute to this company?
This is one of my favourite questions. As far as an employer is concerned, this represents the crux of the whole interview. This is your chance to shine, by saying exactly why you decided to apply for the job. You will need to bring out your particular strengths and show exactly what you can offer. Quoting your experience and skills will help to impress on the employer that you will be a valuable addition to the team. Don't forget to include good points about your personality here.

30. Why are you applying for this post?
This is another variant on the last question and should be answered in the same way.

Dos and don'ts

Do let go! The interviewer wants to get to know who you are, so feel free to be yourself.

Do mind the gap! Make a positive statement about things that would otherwise look negative.

Do speak up for yourself – you have nothing to lose and everything to gain.

Do take care with your appearance; consider every aspect of your presentation.

Do keep your answers simple and clear.

Do speak as you would normally; there is no need to put on an act.

Do boast about your strengths and achievements – all the other candidates will be trying to make themselves look extra good too.

Don't lose your confidence; concentrate on the vacancy that you are interested in.

Don't worry about nerves – they never show to other people as much as you think they do.

Don't smoke or drink tea or coffee in the interview.

Don't assume that the interviewer knows what you are

talking about – the things that you think are obvious may be unclear to others.

Don't give just 'yes' or 'no' answers – the employer will want to know more than that.

Don't use jargon or specialised terms without an explanation.

Don't lie about yourself – you could face dismissal if you obtain a job under false pretences.

Dealing with tricky situations

Starting off the interview

I recommend shaking hands with the interviewer when you enter the room; it shows that you are keen to meet him or her and able to be formally polite. Women sometimes find this difficult, as shaking hands has in the past been more of a male habit. Do not worry if you feel that it would be beyond your capabilities, in a nervous state, to walk in and confidently grasp a stranger's hand, but do respond positively if the interviewer wants to greet you in this way.

You will normally be invited to sit down but, if the interviewer does not mention it, do not immediately assume that he or she is playing some fiendish trick to see how you react under pressure. The much more likely explanation is that he or she has simply forgotten to invite you to be seated, in their concern about which question to ask you first. The solution is to ask politely: 'May I sit down?'

Good manners

On the subject of politeness, you can never be too polite in interviews. On leaving I recommend saying: 'Thank you very much for your time. I have enjoyed meeting you. Goodbye.' Even if you are a habitual smoker, resist the temptation at the interview. Falling ash and smoke surrounding the interviewee never look impressive, even if the employer is smoking.

Some people feel that if they are offered tea or coffee, it is impolite to refuse. But it is best not to accept. In my experience, nervousness only leads to disasters such as the cup falling on the floor or the drink filling the saucer or splashes on your interview suit. Have a strong cup of coffee after the interview is safely over.

If you do not understand or hear a question properly, do not panic. Just ask the questioner to repeat the question. It is better to do this than guess at what was said and make a mistake.

Money

Most jobs give some indication of the salary or wages in the advertisement or job details. If money is not mentioned, avoid discussing the subject at the interview. You will obviously not take any job without knowing what you are going to be paid, but you can always check on this when the interview is over. If you are offered the job, you can say: 'I'm certainly interested in the position, but haven't yet had full details about the conditions of employment. Perhaps you could tell me the salary for the job?'

The interview does not go as planned

If you have planned your responses but do not have the chance to get your points across, you can sometimes hijack the interview so that it goes more in your favour. Suppose that you had not been asked about your strengths, and want to bring in some of the points from your list of ten characteristics. At the end of the interview you could say: 'I would just like to add a brief comment about the sort of person I am' and then say your piece.

Panic sets in

Even the most well-prepared candidate can suffer from temporary drying-up in mid-interview. If your mind goes blank, breathe deeply and play for time by saying something like: 'That's an interesting question.' This allows you a few extra seconds to collect your thoughts. If you are really stuck, ask if you could return to that question later in the interview.

Don't know the answer?

Occasionally, you may be faced with a question that is just too difficult. If you cannot think of anything to say on a subject, explain so simply and without being embarrassed. If possible, indicate that it is an area you are keen to explore.

An excellent book on interviews is *Great Answers to Tough Interview Questions* by Martin John Yate (Kogan Page, 1992).

Chapter 7

Conclusion

'You should not feel rejected just because a pupil decides not to act on your advice immediately – you may prove to have been of great help in the longer run.' Careers teacher

Careers guidance is about helping people to come to terms with their potential and all the opportunities available to them. There are no absolutely correct answers to career problems, only the best solution that can be arrived at and acted on at the time. Your job will be to encourage, help focus and facilitate those decisions.

Quality

As someone who is now involved and interested in the field of careers guidance, you should be keen to keep yourself up to date with new events and information relevant to this discipline. You should try to maintain your level of expertise by reading relevant materials and discussing your work with colleagues whenever possible. In my office, colleagues regularly sit in on each others' interviews with clients in order to see how other team members work. This does necessitate getting the permission of both staff and clients beforehand, but it can prove to be a stimulating exercise, and can help to stop the inevitable complacency and laziness which set in after some time of working alone.

Professional standards

I recommend you join the profession's own association, the Institute of Careers Guidance, at the appropriate level – either as a member, associate or affiliate. The quality of your work will benefit as a result and you will join in a larger movement of people striving to offer the best service they can.

Marketing

Careers guidance has always suffered from being a Cinderella service when compared to its big sister, the world of education. Careers work is often funded on a shoe-string, many areas of the country have no services available for adults and the benefits of careers work are only known to those who have received good careers counselling themselves and the occasional enlightened onlooker. Those of us who are convinced of the importance of the work need to spread the word about the advantages of having comprehensive local provision in every region. We need to broadcast our achievements, open our doors to as many new clients as possible and generally act as missionaries for career development through the guidance process.

Performance indicators

Since vocational guidance started at the beginning of this century, advisers have been trying to prove their worth. The work of giving careers advice involves a lot of grey issues, where different interpretations can be equally appropriate. In a job where it is very difficult to show conclusively exactly how far you have helped people, there is an expectation (and I would say, a responsibility) to collect all the possible evidence to strengthen the claims for the benefits of advice and also to check that you are providing the best service possible.

You may well be required to collect statistics as part of your job but if not, consider implementing ways of measuring success.

This might include a customer satisfaction survey which is given to all clients, asking whether they found the advice given at the interview of use, how they feel about the outcome and whether they would recommend your service to their friends. This could be combined with a follow-up letter to find out where they have ended up. If you can afford reply-paid envelopes or a freepost address, you will dramatically increase the numbers of clients who keep in touch with you after their guidance appointment.

As I mentioned earlier, there are no hard and fast rules about the way to give good guidance, and my advice is certainly not set in stone. To a certain extent an adviser's style depends on his or her own personality and character. Experience will show you the way that you feel most comfortable operating. However, the common-sense guidelines which have been outlined here are useful to follow as a base-line of good practice. There are no definite rights and wrongs about the way to provide careers guidance, only a collection of different views and interpretations to inform our practice. Accordingly, these are my opinions.

Guidance checklist

1. Think through your own appearance and demeanour, the suitability of the environment in which the guidance will occur and make any changes necessary.
2. Strive to be welcoming and ignore your own lack of confidence.
3. Assume nothing that you have not checked out properly.
4. Express any doubts, worries or feelings of embarrassment that you may have.
5. Keep calm, be tolerant and let every client have room to speak and develop.
6. Reserve your judgement but share your impressions.

7. Do not make promises you cannot keep and do not do work for clients that could be more usefully undertaken by the clients themselves.
8. The most common characteristic in clients is a lack of self-confidence, so find as many ways as possible to encourage, boost and inspire the client.
9. Find as many ways as you can to evaluate the worth of what you are doing. Always ask clients what they think of the service and act on good suggestions.
10. Be open to the suggestions and ideas of colleagues and more experienced practitioners.
11. Make improving and updating your work an essential part of the job.
12. Researching and fact-finding are essential parts of your daily work; make time to feel you have enough knowledge to perform in your role properly.
13. Do not feel that you have to be a walking encyclopaedia. The most important thing is to know *where to look* or *who to ask* for the answer.
14. Act as a supportive colleague to others and as a role model to those new to the guidance field.
15. Be careful of the words you use and be aware that they can be interpreted differently from the way they were meant.
16. Broadcast successes to other clients and share good ideas around.
17. Endless analysis is not the name of the game. Help clients to identify and then focus on the important issues.
18. No outcome is not a failure as long as the client feels happy with the situation.
19. Do not expect every client to love you! Do your best and call in a colleague to take over or for more ideas if necessary.
20. Have faith in yourself as one who can offer good guidance to other people.

The key to giving good guidance is in treating the whole of the client and not just concentrating on the problem that they present. In the best traditions of good guidance, I acknowledge the subjective nature of the framework I describe and offer it to help you construct your own initial map only. The journey is up to you. Your clients can only benefit from your interest in the way that you work and I applaud your continuing endeavours to find the best way to give careers advice. Good luck!

> *'Careers advisers act like traffic lights, occasionally saying "stop and check that", sometimes recommending "proceed with caution" and often giving permission by signalling a clear way ahead. The client should be doing the driving but the traffic lights come in very useful and make the journey altogether smoother and less dangerous!'* Ex-head of careers service

Sources of help

UK telephone area codes are due to change on 16 April 1995. The new numbers are given below. Before 16 April 1995 remove the second digit.

For information about working as a careers adviser

The Institute of Careers Guidance (ICG)
27a Lower High Street
Stourbridge
West Midlands DY8 1TA
Tel; 01384 376464

For information about training to become a careers adviser

Local Government Management Board
4th Floor, Arndale House
Arndale Centre
Luton LU1 2TS
Tel; 01582 451166

> *'Careers guidance is about giving impartial advice to identify reasonable routes to the client's preferred option.'* Training adviser working for a training agent

Further Reading from Kogan Page

Books for advisers and their clients

That first step

The A-Z of Careers and Jobs, 6th edition, Diane Burston, 1994
'Provides the perfect starting-point for students and school leavers.' *Education and Training*

Get Qualifications for What You Know You Can Do: A Personal Guide To APL, Susan Simosko, 1992

Getting There: Job Hunting For Women, 2nd edition, Margaret Wallis, 1992

Great Answers to Tough Interview Questions: How to Get the Job You Want, 3rd edition, Martin John Yate, 1992
'The best book on job-hunting generally' *The Financial Times*

How You Can Get That Job!: Application Forms and Letters Made Easy, Rebecca Corfield, 1992
Specifically designed for the inexperienced and less confident applicant.

Interviews Made Easy: How to Get the Psychological Advantage, Mark Parkinson, 1994

The Job-Hunter's Handbook, David Greenwood, 1995
From Acceptance to Zest, David Greenwood covers all the factors that can make job hunting easier or more difficult.

Job Hunting Made Easy: A Step-By-Step Guide, 3rd edition, J Bramham and D Cox, 1995

Job Sharing: A Practical Guide, Pam Walton, 1991

Offbeat Careers: 60 Ways to Avoid becoming an Accountant, 3rd edition, Vivien Donald, 1995
Sixty alternative careers, each described in full, with details of contact name, necessary skills and likely earnings.

Preparing Your Own CV, Rebecca Corfield, 1990
'Invaluable ... Well worth reading' *International Journal of Career Management*

Successful Interview Skills: How to Present Yourself With Confidence, Rebecca Corfield, 1990

Test Your Own Aptitude, 2nd edition, J Barrett and G Williams, 1995
Anyone seeking a job can match their abilities, personality and motivation to a list of over 400 careers.

Your Job Search, P Gaudet, M Estier and E Riera, 1993

Moving on

Changing Your Job after 35: The Daily Telegraph Guide, 7th edition, Godfrey Golzen and Philip Plumbley, 1993

The Expatriate's Handbook: Getting the Best Out of Overseas Employment, B Twinn and P Burns, 1993

How to Get a Job After 45: The Daily Telegraph Guide, 2nd edition, Julie Bayley, 1992

How to Succeed in a Highly Competitive Job Market: A Workbook for Executives, Brian Croucher, 1994
The ideal book for job-seeking professionals.

The Image Factor: A Guide to Effective Self-Presentation for Career Enhancement, Eleri Sampson, 1994
This book shows how an appropriate image can have a powerful influence on the development of any career.

The Job Assault Course: The Guide to Civilian Employment forrm Service Personnel, M C Lindsay Stewart, 1992

Manage Your Own Career: A Self-Help Guide to Career Choice and Change, Ben Ball, 1989

The Mid Career Action Guide: A Practical Guide to Mid Career

Change, 2nd edition, Derek Kemp and Fred Kemp, 1992
Illustrates the potential for change and self-advancement. Practical employment alternatives are put forward, together with contact names and addresses.

Working Abroad: The Daily Telegraph Guide to Living and Working Overseas, 17th edition, Godfrey Golzen, 1994
'Covers all aspects of expatriate life' *Personnel Today*

Selection and recruitment tests

How to Pass Computer Selection Tests, Sanjay Modha, 1994
How to Pass Graduate Recruitment Tests, Mike Bryon, 1994
How to Pass Selection Tests, Mike Bryon and Sanjay Modha, 1991
How to Pass Technical Selection Tests, Mike Bryon and Sanjay Modha, 1993

Kogan Page Careers Series

'Essential information at affordable prices'
Times Education Supplement

These 27 practical and inexpensive books are packed with useful information and sound advice on a wide variety of professions and careers, from accountancy to working with young people. Written by experts, the books are essential reading for all careers advisers, school and college leavers, graduates or anyone considering a career change.

Index